Talking to Your Children About God

Talking to Your
Children
About GOD

RICK OSBORNE

HarperSanFrancisco
A Division of HarperCollins*Publishers*

TALKING TO YOUR CHILDREN ABOUT GOD. Copyright © 1998 by Rick Osborne. All rights reserved. Printed in the United States of America. No part of this book may be used or reproduced in any manner whatsoever without written permission except in the case of brief quotations embodied in critical articles and reviews. For information address HarperCollins Publishers, 10 East 53rd Street, New York, NY 10022.

HarperCollins books may be purchased for educational, business, or sales promotional use. For information please write: Special Markets Department, HarperCollins Publishers, Inc., 10 East 53rd Street, New York, NY 10022.

HarperCollins Web site: http://www.harpercollins.com

HarperCollins®, 📖 ®, and HarperSanFrancisco™ are trademarks of HarperCollins Publishers, Inc.

FIRST EDITION

Library of Congress Cataloging-in-Publication Data
Osborne, Rick.
    Talking to your children about God / Rick Osborne.—1st ed.
        p.   cm.
    ISBN 0–06–066751–6 (pbk.)
    1. Christian education—Home training. I. Title.
BV1590.073 1998   98–12649
248.8′45—dc21

98 99 00 01 02 ❖/RRD(H) 10 9 8 7 6 5 4 3 2 1

Contents

Let's Talk Religion   **1**

  A. Since having children, I think a lot more about God and spiritual issues. Do all parents go through this?   6

  B. Can we teach our children about God and give them a good moral upbringing without going too far and becoming weird?   9

  C. How important is it to teach children about spiritual things? Won't they learn on their own when they're older?   14

  D. How can I teach my kids about God when I don't know much about the Bible and my own spiritual life is shaky at best?   17

1. God   **19**

  A. Can my children know who God is and what he's really like?   20

  B. How can I explain "a relationship with God" to my children?   25

  C. How can I motivate my children to want to learn about God?   29

  D. How can I explain to my children what God's character is like?   33

  E. How can I answer my children's questions about such things as God's omnipotence and the Trinity?   44

  F. How can I help my children have a strong faith in God?   51

2. The Bible   61

A. How can I show my children that the Bible is trustworthy?   62

B. What kind of Bible or Bible storybook should I use with my children?   72

C. How can I tell my kids in a simple way what the Bible is all about?   76

D. What can I do to help my kids get a handle on how all the pieces of the Bible fit together?   88

E. What are some practical tips for reading the Bible to or with my kids?   97

F. How can I help my kids read through the Bible?   106

G. Is there value in having my kids memorize verses from the Bible?   114

3. Church   117

A. Can I raise good kids who believe in God without taking them to church?   118

B. What's the purpose of church, and how can it help my children?   124

C. Isn't there a right and a wrong way for a church to believe and teach? Is it important to take my children to a certain church?   136

D. My spouse and I come from different church backgrounds. How can we agree on where to take the children to church?   142

E. What about special services for children, such as baptism, dedication, and confirmation? Are these an important part of my children's spiritual development?   145

4. Prayer   **149**

  A. How can I explain to my children what
     prayer is?   150

  B. How important is it for my children to kneel
     and fold their hands and close their eyes?   154

  C. How can I help my children's prayers grow
     with them so that they don't grow *out* of them?   158

  D. What things should I be encouraging my
     children to pray about?   164

  E. Are memorized prayers important, and are
     they effective?   171

  F. How do I explain things to my children
     when their prayers aren't answered?   175

5. Angels and Heaven   **181**

  A. How can I answer my kids' questions about
     angels?   182

  B. What can I tell my kids about heaven?   187

Conclusion   **195**

  Can we be sure our prayers and efforts
  will help?   195

Acknowledgments

Although only my name appears on the cover of this book, it's not the only one that deserves to be there. The process that eventually puts a book in the reader's hand takes a team of talented people, all doing their part. It also involves many people who over the years contribute to the author's life and growth—a process that directly affects the content and the author's ability to write the book.

I would like to acknowledge my agents, Michael Carlisle and Matthew Bialer, for their encouragement and persistence; all the people at Harper San Francisco who worked on this book, but especially Mark Chimsky for his ideas and for making the process enjoyable; and my team at Lightwave.

I would also like to acknowledge the list of people, too long to name individually, who have contributed to the contents of this book by contributing to my life. And I would like to acknowledge in a special way my friend Ed van der Maas, who has contributed to this book in both ways, by helping me with the manuscript and by contributing to my life and growth.

Let's Talk Religion

~~~~~~

A. Since having children, I think a lot more about God and spiritual issues. Do all parents go through this?

B. Can we teach our children about God and give them a good moral upbringing without going too far and becoming weird?

C. How important is it to teach children about spiritual things? Won't they learn on their own when they're older?

D. How can I teach my kids about God when I don't know much about the Bible and my own spiritual life is shaky at best?

~~~~~~

Not too many years ago, three topics were taboo in polite conversation and at dinner parties: sex, politics, and religion. In the sixties the topic of sex started coming out of the closet, and today it's pretty much out in the open, sitting down comfortably with us at the dinner table.

Politics, too, has become a staple of polite conversation. People stopped believing in the perfect political party and the perfect politician long ago. In the absence of such belief, politics seems to have become a matter of *us* against *them*—the voters against the politicians. Since we're now all more or less on the same side, we don't mind talking about political issues. Unless, of course, a politician has been invited to our dinner party, in which case the taboo still applies—not because an argument will ensue but because no one wants to get the politician started!

Which leaves the third topic, the granddaddy of all conversation killers: religion. For years this last holdout has been trying desperately to get out of the closet. It's not that God and faith aren't important to us. We just have a hard time talking about them. Polls taken to measure our spiritual temperature in 1997 show that, of the people interviewed,

- 97% pray at least once a week or more often.
- 95% believe in God.
- 91% believe that Jesus Christ died on the cross.
- 89% believe that Jesus Christ was the Son of God.
- 85% believe that the Bible is the Word of God.
- 79% believe that when people pray for God's help in healing someone with a disease considered incurable by medical science, sometimes God answers.
- 76% attend church or other religious services at least weekly.
- 76% pray as a means of coping with physical or emotional problems.[1]

_____

[1] Summary report of faith in America provided for Lightwave Publishing by the Roper Center, Univ. of Conn. (Storrs, Conn.), 1997. That report cites findings from the following: the *Washington Post*,

Faith and religion are such a major part of who we are in America that it's amazing how long we've felt uncomfortable talking openly about our beliefs. Today, we're finally willing to have religion come out of the closet—in fact, the doors have been ripped off the closet, and we're all looking expectantly inside.

Here's a quote from a recent article that appeared in our local newspaper, the *Vancouver Sun:*

> "God is hot." That's how Roy Larson, head of the Center for Religion and the News Media, described the 1990's surge of fascination with things spiritual. Larson, who is with Northwestern University, told a group of religion writers in Chicago . . . that God's rediscovered renown has not yet peaked in North America.
>
> The signs of God's hotness are everywhere. At the Chicago conference, I learned dozens of newspapers across North America are expanding their religion sections. TV stations are hiring religion reporters. Giant charitable foundations, like Ford, Pew and Lilly, are pumping tens of millions of dollars into advancing religious understanding through various media. The most startling evidence of God's new sizzle is in book publishing. Lynn Garrett, religion editor of *Publishers Weekly,* told us that the publishing industry has recently been transformed by the amazing rise in sales of "R/S/I books" (which stands for "Religion/Spirituality/Inspiration"). Such books now make up the number-one genre in publishing.

Before we could openly talk about sex, we as a society had to reexamine how we felt about it. And that's what we're doing today with spirituality and religion. But we're discovering that

with interviewing conducted by ICR Survey Research Group, July 11, 1997; the Luntz Research Companies for CASA, July 7, 1997; an ABC News poll, Mar. 28, 1997; and Princeton Survey Research Associates for *Newsweek,* Mar. 22, 1997.

religion has been in the closet for so long, and we're surrounded by so many religious options, that we're not really
sure what it is that we're all peering into the closet to find.

Perhaps we're uncomfortable discussing religion for that
very reason. We know (or suspect) that there's something to
what we believe, but because as we grew up we were taught
so little about what we believe—let alone *why* we believe—our
spiritual and religious concepts seem impractical and disconnected from reality and from our day-to-day lives. We hesitate
to discuss religion because we're aware that we don't really
understand what we're talking about, and who wants to
admit that—even though the vast majority of us are in the
same boat? Besides, we can talk about sex and politics objec-
tively, but when we begin talking seriously about religion,
spirituality, and faith, we risk letting people see our most personal and vulnerable side—another thing we tend to avoid.

In reading through hundreds of questions and comments
from regular parents in preparation for this book, I found
that many parents remember their own childhood religious
experience as being boring, having little practical importance
or effect, and leaving them with more questions than answers.
Their main question now is, What can we do to change this
pattern with our own children?

> **Many parents remember their own childhood religious experience as being boring, having little practical importance or effect, and leaving them with more questions than answers. Their main question now is, What can we do to change this pattern with our own children?**

Every parent suspects that
we end up parenting the same
way that we were parented.
And that will indeed happen—
unless we purposely learn and
apply a different approach.
We'll follow the same patterns
we ourselves experienced if we
don't open ourselves up to new
patterns and become willing
to travel by a different parent-
ing compass. This need for openness to new approaches is
also—perhaps *especially*—true of faith.

The purpose of this book is to help you come alongside your children, and together with them take apart what you believe, examine it, and put it back together in a way that they can understand. As we help our children grow up understanding what they believe, why they believe it, and how they can practically live it, the third and final conversation stopper will be forced out of the closet.

Since having children, I think a lot more about God and spiritual issues. Do all parents go through this?

Parenting magazine teamed up with Gallup for a survey called "The Parenting Religion Poll."[2] Here are some of the results:

- Almost 90% of parents have talked to their children about God.
- 64% of families say grace at meals.
- 64% of mothers and fathers say bedtime prayers with their children.

---

[2] "The Parenting Religion Poll." Parenting, Dec./Jan. 1996, 123.

You've probably heard the saying "There are no atheists in foxholes." Judging by the findings of the *Parenting* poll, I think there aren't many in the trenches of parenting either. Consider these additional statistics:

- Regardless of their income, education, gender, marital status, or occupation, 95% of parents believe in God.
- 40% of parents say that religion has become more important since they had children.

For years experts have agreed that children have a natural tendency toward faith and belief in God. The same now also appears to be true of us as parents. The miracle of childbirth and the wonder of watching a unique person grow and take shape is more than enough to stir up the natural tendency toward faith that's in all of us. And what's more, we as parents seem to have a deep-seated desire to help our children grow up with faith in God.

Our children instinctively and naturally want and need food to live, and we as parents have a corresponding natural desire to feed our children. (It's a good thing that God gave us this desire, or we'd probably never get through the spaghetti-dumping stage.) The same is true of spiritual food: our children instinctively and naturally want it and need it to live long, happy, and complete lives, and placed within us is the corresponding desire to give our children that spiritual food.

There's an example of this in the biblical record of Jesus' life. Here's what happened when some parents listened to their hearts and took their children to see Jesus:

> The wonder of watching a unique person grow and take shape is more than enough to stir up the natural tendency toward faith that's in all of us. And what's more, we as parents seem to have a deep-seated desire to help our children grow up with faith in God.

People were also bringing babies to Jesus. They wanted him to touch them. When the disciples saw this, they told the people to stop. But Jesus asked the children to come to him. "Let the little children come to me," he said. "Don't keep them away. God's kingdom belongs to people like them. What I'm about to tell you is true. Anyone who will not receive God's kingdom like a little child will never enter it."

(LUKE 18:15–17)

Jesus recognized the obvious desire of the parents, but he also recognized and responded directly to the desire of the children and called them to himself: "Let the little children come to me."

Our children were created as *God's* children and have everything they need to respond to his love. God has given us the awesome privilege and the desire to point them in the right direction and to help them discover and respond to that love.

But although the desire is there, the actual process—which can be quite down-to-earth—takes some doing. Children's natural desire for food, and our corresponding desire to nourish, helps get the food in their stomachs eventually, but getting them through that spaghetti-dumping, food-flinging, hands-are-mini-food-processors stage takes time and training. Feeding our children's spirit—getting them past the sibling-thumping, question-flinging, hands-are-windmills-smacking-our-face-while-we're-trying-to-pray-with-them stage—also takes time and training.

> Feeding our children's spirit—getting them past the sibling-thumping, question-flinging, hands-are-windmills-smacking-our-face-while-we're-trying-to-pray-with-them stage—takes time and training.

Jesus rewarded those who brought their children to him by receiving their children. But he went on to say, with all those parents listening, "I tell you the truth, anyone who will not receive the kingdom of God like a little child will never enter it." In the process of helping our children respond to their natural desire for faith, we ourselves are reawakened by watching them respond and are inspired to return to or maintain a simple, honest, childlike faith ourselves.

Can we teach our children about God and give them a good moral upbringing without going too far and becoming weird?

Imagine someone discovering, in a collection of old, dusty books, the greatest cookbook ever written. Fame of the book spreads, and soon clubs, groups, and even entire societies embrace this cookbook as *their* cookbook and begin to use it as their primary culinary guide.

After a while this much-revered book becomes so popular that select groups of specialists are formed to examine when and how it was written, who wrote it, and what the motivation behind its creation was. They explore its minutest details and build grand theories to explain the greatness of the book. They publish books and articles and hold conventions. Some become famous for their praise of the great work, others for their criticism.

But because even the experts can't agree on its origin or purpose or on how to use it correctly, the cookbook becomes too intimidating for anybody else to read, let alone use. So the cookbook begins to gather dust on everyone's shelves, although the stories of its wonderful, life-enhancing recipes are still circulated, and those who are considered the keepers of the cookbook gather everybody together once a week and talk at great length about how wonderful the book is and how lucky the people are to have the recipes.

But the people who attend those gatherings sometimes wonder what all the talk has to do with their cooking, which isn't going very well. Frankly, they could use a lot of help with it. But they keep coming every week, even though what they hear is rather disconnected from their everyday breakfast-lunch-and-dinner life, because it seems right and somehow holy, a beautiful tradition they want to keep.

What comes to mind when we think of the place of religion in our society? Often the image we see is that of a system more or less disconnected from or above real life, a somehow holy and beautiful tradition that's simply out of touch with today's reality.

It's strange that our faith and the images that accompany it have become so distant and detached from our lives that when we need advice for everyday concerns we often look everywhere except there.

On the other hand, when we think about daily life and how to live it, about how to get along with others, how to be successful and happy, how to make it in life, how to be the right kind of person, how to love and be loved, how to have a good marriage, how to be popular, how to handle money, how to like yourself, and so on, what comes to mind? Counselors, gurus, and motivational speakers. Every time you turn on the television or the radio or open up a newspaper or a magazine, someone has a new system or more advice on how to live life: eight laws for this and six steps to that, the keys to this and the secrets to that. Everyone is jumping around, looking for the wisdom that will finally put their life on track and make them successful.

It's strange that our faith and the images that accompany it have become so distant and detached from our lives that when we need advice for everyday concerns we often look everywhere *except* there.

> **Jesus spent very little time talking about doctrine and lofty theological concepts, about things that only the intellectually gifted can grasp. He spent his time teaching about life and how to live it.**

Nobody ever accused Jesus of being lofty or talking about things that had nothing to do with life. Jesus talked with regular people like you and me, and he talked about things that matter in everyday life. He was so down-to-earth that the religious leaders had difficulty accepting him. They accused him of being "a drunkard, a friend of tax collectors and sinners," of being the kind of person they, as religious leaders, didn't want to associate with.

If you examine Jesus' teaching from start to finish, you'll see that he spent very little time talking about doctrine and lofty theological concepts, about things that only the intellectually gifted can grasp. He spent his time teaching his disciples, and all who would listen, about life and how to live it: how to live with God and with others, how to love, how to share and be generous, how to show mercy, how to get along and be a friend, how to handle finances, how to be happy and at peace, how to have a good marriage, and how to receive God's provision, care, and blessings. Even when Jesus spoke about things that seem abstract—things like prayer and faith—he talked about them in the context of daily life, showing how they work in practice and how they make life work better. Jesus said, "I have come so they can have life. I want them to have it in the fullest possible way" (John 10:10).

Jesus didn't come to start a religion. He came to restore us to our loving Heavenly Father, who wants, in every way, to demonstrate his love for us and give us the life that he created us to have!

> **Jesus didn't come to start a religion. He came to restore us to our loving Heavenly Father, who wants, in every way, to demonstrate his love for us and give us the life that he created us to have!**

God didn't intend our faith to be a strange, mystical appendage to our lives, or merely a splash of tradition and beauty that, when added to the overall mix of our life, somehow makes it more meaningful.

He intended faith to be the *foundation* of our lives, the structure that supports everything else. Christianity isn't a religion in the sense of a collection of forms and traditions to follow. It isn't merely a creed or a set of beliefs. It's a *way of life*, a code rather than a creed. It's the restoration of the gift of life and instructions for making life work the way God created it to work.

Teaching our children about God and passing the basics of the Christian faith on to them isn't and shouldn't be weird. Yes, we should try to help them understand our traditions and the particular way in which we express and celebrate our faith. But more important, we need to introduce them to God, to his love and his recipe for a great life. We should help them find the love of God as their foundation and as the key to the awesome life that God intends for them—a life filled with meaning and purpose.

What, you ask, happened to the society with the revered cookbook? A lot of people kept struggling with their cooking, and when they needed help they watched the many culinary gurus who had sprung up and were now doing infomercials

> **God intended faith to be the foundation of our lives, the structure that supports everything else.**

and guest appearances on the shopping channel, and they bought many wonderful books and gadgets that promised a lot but delivered little (charging them all to their credit cards).

But some people started reading the cookbook again and found that it wasn't complicated at all. They cautiously tried one or two of the recipes and discovered that, though simple, the instructions made their cooking phenomenal. And they began to teach their children the recipes so that they would know how to be great cooks. And cooking became a favorite topic of conversation.

How important is it to teach children about spiritual things? Won't they learn on their own when they're older?

If math and reading are important for our kids' future, how much more crucial is the foundation: faith. Being able to read books and balance a checkbook makes life easier, but it doesn't answer the big questions that give life meaning and context.

Who am I? Why am I here? Is there a God? Is there a purpose for my life?

These are the *big* questions we ask when life goes wrong or doesn't make sense, when we're searching for answers and have to make decisions, when we want to know where to go and what to do with our lives. We ask these questions because we need and are searching for a *context* for our lives that will help give us direction, purpose, and hope. But often we end up setting the questions aside as being too lofty and philosophical to be of practical value in our everyday lives.

The truth is that God has provided us with simple, practical answers to the big questions—answers that are essential to life as God created it because they give our lives context. Talking to our children about God and teaching them the basics of the faith helps them begin to understand these answers on their own level. This understanding then helps them live their lives with confidence, purpose, and direction—even when times are tough. It gives them context.

- When your child asks, "Who am I?" the answer that builds self-respect and a proper self-image and gives his or her life context is, "You're a child of God, created in his image with dignity. You're unique, created specifically, purposely, and specially by God and loved by him as an individual. You're treated and cared for by him as a dearly loved member of his family for all eternity."

If we go through life with no image, or a negative image, of who we are, we end up not becoming all that we could be. When our children can confidently answer the question "Who am I?" with God's answer, they're propelled forward with the strength to build and grow and overcome fear, rejection, and setbacks.

- When your child asks, "Why am I here?" the answer that gives his or her life context and meaning is, "You're here because God loves you and wanted to give you life, a life that's rich with love and relationship with him and with others. You were created completely unique, and you have special and unique value that you can bring to others in this world."

When children—or anyone, for that matter—are convinced of their value, they take a valuable place in life, succeeding at what they do and helping others in the process.

- When your child asks, "Is there a purpose for my life?" the answer that provides solid ground to march forward on is, "God has uniquely gifted you, given you talents, a special aptitude, and a personality that together make you an individual. He wants to teach and direct you, advise and guide you into the perfect spot for you in time and in the world, so that you'll be fulfilled and your life will make a difference."

Many of us take a long, long time to find our place in life; indeed, many *never* find it. If we don't understand that God has a purpose for our life, we try to shape a life without God, and we end up empty. If our children understand that God has a purpose for them and for their lives, that understanding will cause them to trust him and look to him for growth, guidance, and direction.

- When your child asks, "Is there a God? " the answer—which all of us already know in our hearts—is the foundation for all of the awesome things that give our lives meaning: truth, love, purpose, individual uniqueness and value, hope, and faith. By talking to our children about God, we give them a real purpose, a solid foundation, and a true meaning for their lives.

Trusting God and doing things his way isn't always easy, and it doesn't guarantee that our children won't go through difficult and sometimes unexplainable things in their lives. But when their lives have context, when they know why they're here and who they are, who God is and what he wants for them, they'll have the strength and sense of value and purpose they need to keep on trusting and to keep on doing things God's way. We can trust that God will work everything out to the good (Romans 8:28).

How can I teach my kids about God when I don't know much about the Bible and my own spiritual life is shaky at best?

I BROUGHT DAD'S PILLOW, SO WHEN HE FALLS ASLEEP HIS HEAD WON'T BANG ON THE PEW LIKE LAST WEEK.

Many of us feel that our own lack of understanding, or the fact that we struggle with our own spiritual life and relationship with God, will prevent us from successfully teaching our kids about God. Surprisingly, the opposite may be true.

Let me illustrate with the well-known Old Testament story of the Exodus from Egypt. The Israelites who left Egypt under Moses were anything but the perfect picture of strong faith and spiritual understanding. They were "stiffnecked" (stubborn) and ended up wandering around in the wilderness for forty years because they had trouble trusting God and doing things his way.

But—and this is what's surprising—their children grew up to be one of the most outstanding examples of a generation of Israelites who got it right. They successfully took the

Promised Land. They consistently followed God and his principles and for the most part enjoyed successful lives.

Their kids, on the other hand—the third generation—went right back to being like the generation that left Egypt. The stubborn, stiffnecked Israelites raised a generation of kids who got it right, and the generation that got it right raised kids who messed up royally.

Perhaps the best way for us to teach our children about God and following his ways is to grow with them.

When I first saw this piece of history, I found it confusing. It would seem logical that parents who know, trust, and follow God would have kids who do the same, while parents who don't would have children who don't. What's the explanation? It's that the stubborn, stiffnecked Israelites didn't stay that way. The story shows that they began to learn and to grow and to change. Although they often got it wrong, they were continually moving in the right direction, and their children saw the results of bad choices and the results of good choices. Those children grew up seeing their parents struggle and grow with God.

But when they themselves grew up, they got comfortable in their relationship with God and failed to teach their children about him, probably assuming that understanding would happen automatically.

The encouragement in this story is that perhaps the best way for us to teach our children about God and following his ways is to grow with them. Sometimes we think that in order to teach our children spiritual things we need to be perfect. But our children live with us; they know we're *far* from perfect! And even if we're doing well, we should never stop growing. As we trust God to change and lead us, we can share with our children what we learned and how we learned it, and they can grow with us.

If, as you read this, you find yourself in the position of that first generation of Israelites, talk to God and ask him to help you learn and grow and to give you the wisdom to help your children do the same, alongside you.

1
·
God

~~~~~~

A. Can my children know who God is and what he's really like?

B. How can I explain "a relationship with God" to my children?

C. How can I motivate my children to want to learn about God?

D. How can I explain to my children what God's character is like?

E. How can I answer my children's questions about such things as God's omnipotence and the Trinity?

F. How can I help my children have a strong faith in God?

~~~~~~

Can my children know who God is and what he's really like?

Before we can help our children relate to God, we first have to give them an accurate picture of who God is. Once they understand who God is and what he's like, they won't find it hard to relate to him.

It's easy to give kids an entirely wrong idea of God. For example, we're afraid our children will do the wrong thing, and we know that we can't be there to watch their every step. Using God as a Heavenly Baby-sitter, we may tell our children that God is always watching and that he knows when they do something wrong. Then they begin to see God as the Big Eye in the Sky, a cosmic killjoy.

So—who *is* God, and what's he really like?

We don't get much of a clue from our society. When something really terrible happens—an earthquake, a flood, or a volcanic eruption—we call it "an act of God." But when some-one calls a good and unexpectedly awesome event a miracle or an answer to prayer, many people mock the explanation, others work hard to explain the event away rationally, and most of us merely doubt in silence (if we give the matter much thought at all). God is useful for blame, but he doesn't have much of a credit rating.

The dictionary isn't much help either when it defines God as "the supreme being, seen as the omnipotent creator and ruler of the universe." This definition may well be technically correct—it's so vague that it would be difficult for it to be wrong—but what does it really tell us about God? It tells us *what* God is, but not *who* God is. Webster's definition no more paints a correct picture of who God is than the definition "sentient mammalian biped, in-habitant of the sphere called earth" describes who *you* are, although it does say something about *what* you are.

> God is useful for blame, but he doesn't have much of a credit rating.

None of us likes being treated like a number, like just another bipedal mammal. Each of us is a unique person. We want to be loved, recognized, and valued as individuals, as *who* we are rather than *what* we are. God is also a unique per-son, with a unique personality. We were made like him—"in his image," as the Bible says. Picturing God only as "the supreme being" or thinking of him as the unreachable, unknowable "creator and ruler of the universe" ignores who God is—it ignores God as a *person*. I doubt that he likes that sort of treatment any better than we do.

But even when we acknowledge that God is a person, we sometimes show by the way we communicate with him that he's a stranger to us. We think that we can talk only *to* God, not *with* him. And we think that we should talk with him only about serious and important things—that is, things *we* think are serious and important. We feel that when we talk to God we have to be on our best behavior. We think that we should talk to God only in a certain way—in solemn tones and maybe even in Elizabethan language full of words like *goeth* and *knowest* and *thee* and *thou*. We may also think it's necessary to speak and act differently when we go to church—as if God didn't know what we're really like.

All these things demonstrate that by and large we really don't know who God is and what he's like. Which takes us back to the original question: Can we teach our children who God is and what he's really like?

> Picturing God only as "the supreme being" or thinking of him as the unreachable, unknowable "creator and ruler of the universe" ignores who God is—it ignores God as a *person*.

The answer is yes! But that teaching isn't found in religious abstractions and discussions about God. It's found in the life of Jesus. His life was God's show-and-tell. Jesus didn't come to discuss religion. He came to restore us to our Heavenly Father by showing us through his life who God is and what God is truly like.

When Jesus was praying for his disciples just before his death, he said, "Father, you are holy. . . . I have shown you to them" (John 17:25–26). Earlier he had said that anyone who had seen him had seen the Father (John 14:9) and that everything he did and everything he said was what the Father gave him to do and say. Jesus' life, character, and actions were a perfect demonstration of who God is. As the author of the book of Hebrews put it, Jesus is "the exact likeness of God's being" (Hebrews 1:3).

Jesus didn't go around acting like the fuzzy image that pops into our heads when we read "the supreme being, seen as the omnipotent creator and ruler of the universe." He was very approachable, extremely understanding, kind, compassionate, and forgiving.

> Jesus didn't come to discuss religion. He came to restore us to our Heavenly Father by showing us through his life who God is and what God is truly like.

Jesus didn't cause floods or earthquakes or set off volcanic eruptions. In fact, he reprimanded his disciples for even suggesting that they should call fire down from heaven to destroy some people who wouldn't welcome them into their village (Luke 9:52–55). God's true character and compassion were demonstrated in what Jesus did. He healed the sick, fed the hungry, gave to the poor, encouraged the troubled, prayed for the children, and taught anybody and everybody who would listen about God's love.

And no one who came to Jesus needed to talk and act differently than they normally did. Jesus lived with, taught, and related to regular people like you and me. He showed us by example how God relates to people. That's why prayer can and should be sincere and honest—real communication that comes from the heart.

But what about sin? Jesus didn't go around trying to catch people in sin so he could tell them how bad they were and how God would punish them. That's what the religious leaders were good at doing. Jesus came to show that God wants to *forgive,* not condemn. Jesus came to die for us, not to condemn us.

When the religious leaders brought a woman who had been caught in the act of adultery to Jesus to see if he would consent to having her stoned to death, as required by the Law of Moses, he told the people who had gathered,

> "Has any one of you not sinned? Then you be the first to throw a stone at her."

After everyone had left, Jesus said,

> "Woman, where are they? Hasn't anyone found you guilty?"
> "No one, sir," she said.
> "Then I don't find you guilty either," Jesus said. "Go now and leave your life of sin."
>
> (JOHN 8:3–11)

Jesus painted by his actions a very accurate picture of who God is, what he's like, how he responds to us, and how he gets involved in our lives—a picture that's as different from how our society generally views God as a Rembrandt is from a paint-by-numbers picture.

Introducing your children to God with the straightforward and loving picture that Jesus painted is a relatively simple task—especially compared to the task of trying to introduce them to "the supreme being, seen as the omnipotent creator and ruler of the universe"!

God's true character and compassion were demonstrated in what Jesus did. He healed the sick, fed the hungry, gave to the poor, encouraged the troubled, prayed for the children, and taught anybody and everybody who would listen about God's love.

How can I explain "a relationship with God" to my children?

The most effective way to teach and train children anything is to help them understand *why* you're teaching them and *how* you plan to do it, and to proceed not by simply telling them what you want them to learn and do but by working with them and making learning a joint responsibility. The first step is the big picture. Your children need to know that you love them, that you want them to have the best possible life, and that it's therefore your job to teach them, train them, discipline them, and help them grow in every area so that they can have that good life. If they understand your motivation, they won't feel that you're just someone put on earth to make them miserable every time you try to help them grow in a particular area.

By way of illustration, let's tackle the mess that our kids call a room—about as down-to-earth as you can get. Children are generally convinced that the reason you nag them about their room is because you're a hopeless neat-freak who doesn't know how to relax. And the whole issue tends to become a battle of wills: you think the room should be clean; they think it doesn't matter.

But if you take the time to explain and to train—to tell them how important it is to learn to clean up after themselves and organize their space as a life habit, and *why* those things are important—you can get your children to see that you're all on the same side, working together. You might explain, for example, that cleaning as they go is easier, saves time, and makes life more pleasant. Furthermore, by learning to organize and clean their room, they'll begin to develop the life skills of organization and discipline that will help them in every area of life. Those skills will add value to who they are as employees, spouses, and friends, gaining them the appreciation and respect of the people in their lives. Explain to them that if we learn valuable life skills while our responsibilities are small, then life is easier to conquer as the responsibilities grow.

Of course, some six-year-olds won't be profoundly impressed by a payoff that, from their perspective, might as well be a million years in the future—the promise that the skills learned from cleaning their room will "add value to who they are as employees, spouses, and friends, gaining them the appreciation and respect of the people in their lives." The focus of your explanation will therefore obviously be different when you're talking with a six-year-old than when you discuss this issue with a teenager. Equally important, your explanation must be adapted to each kid's individual personality.

But regardless of age or personality, the basic point remains the same: once the picture is painted properly and your children see that the training is for their sake and not yours, they're able to join in and develop their own motivation and sense of responsibility for the process.

Let's move from messy rooms back to spiritual growth and development. The same foundational parenting principle applies here as well: your children need to know that there's a reason, a purpose, a goal, and a benefit to building their spiritual life. (Actually, it's easier to explain a relationship with God and have your children respond to his love than it is to explain the reasons and benefits for keeping their bedroom clean and have them respond to your gentle but ever-so-persistent reminders.)

The first thing we need to explain to our children is *why* they need to develop a relationship with God. Without that explanation, our children can get the idea that the whole activity is just some religious thing that you want them to do so that they'll behave themselves.

We need to explain to our children that God wants to be the most awesome loving Father they can possibly imagine. He wants to help them in every way possible. Have your children imagine the benefits of being a child of the richest, most powerful, and wisest person who ever lived—who also happens to be the greatest parent who ever lived.

> It's easier to explain a relationship with God and have your children respond to his love than it is to explain the reasons and benefits for keeping their bedroom clean.

This means that we also need to let our children know that God created us with the right to choose and the ability to learn and grow, to excel and succeed. God didn't make us robots. He created us as his children, with dignity and honor. But with that dignity and privilege comes the responsibility to learn and to grow.

God created many parts of life in which we, like artists, are free to express individuality and personal differences and tastes. But in order for our lives to be secure and happy, he created many things that are foundational, that give our lives a framework. Gravity isn't just a nice idea; it's a law without which life couldn't function. Yes, it limits the directions in which we can fall to a single one: down. But it's that very limitation that keeps us from having to float after anything we happen to let go of, freeing us up to do more important things.

Similarly, God has given foundational principles for things like behavior, attitude, character, and relationships—rules that, if adhered to, free us up to be the best persons we can be. He wants us to learn and understand these principles so that we can experience the awesome privilege that he gave us when he created us—for us to be his children and for him to be our Father. His plan wasn't to create us and then disappear; his plan was to be with us and to help us learn and grow, achieve and be happy. He gave us life, but he also gave us himself as our Father so that we could learn from him. After all, we're made like him.

How can I motivate my children to want to learn about God?

THE TWO CATS AND DOGS WILL HAVE TO DO! THIS OBJECT LESSON HAS GONE FAR ENOUGH.

Children, obey your parents as believers in the Lord. Obey them because it's the right thing to do. Scripture says, "Honor your father and mother." That is the first commandment that has a promise. "Then things will go well with you. You will live a long time on the earth."

(EPHESIANS 6:1–3)

For almost two thousand years now, these verses have been a favorite passage of Scripture for every parent who's ever read the Bible. Unfortunately, when we examine the context, we see that these verses *aren't* telling our children that if they agree to do everything we say and make our lives wonderful, God will somehow reward them with a good and long life.

The Apostle Paul quoted these verses, with a few minor changes, from the Old Testament. In their original context, Moses was reading God's Law to the Israelites after they left Egypt and before they entered the Promised Land, Canaan. He told the people that if they lived God's way, they would enjoy a long life in the land of Canaan. The adults who listened to Moses (and later to Joshua) all agreed to do things God's way.

The adults were also told to teach their children God's principles, and that too they agreed to do. The children were told to honor and obey their parents, but they were told this *in the context of their parents' agreement* to follow God's principles and to teach those principles to their children. And the children were promised that they would receive the same thing as their parents for following God—a long and happy life in the Promised Land.

Paul updated the quote by adding the words "in the Lord"—"Children, obey your parents as believers *in the Lord*"— to show that, just as in the original context, the command still assumes a willingness to do things God's way, on the part of the adults as well as the children.

The interesting thing to note in the verses just quoted is that God has given us the way to motivate children and to help them *want* to learn about him and follow him. And that motivator isn't fear. We need to be careful not to try to motivate our children to love God and to do things his way by using fear—whether fear of hell or of some other punishment. Fear repels, while love draws. God says, "I have loved you with a love that lasts forever. I have kept on loving you with faithful love" (Jeremiah 31:3). Paul points to the *promise* that goes with the commandment: "Then things will go well with you. You will live a long time on the earth." The way to motivate is positive: God's way is the way life works best; following and applying God's principles is the key to a happy and successful life.

The Apostle John wrote, "God is love"—that is, God doesn't just *feel* or *have* love for us; he *is* love. God's core motivation for *everything* that he says and does is love—the kind of love that's completely unselfish and expresses itself by giving. (It's the love often referred to by the Greek word *agape*.) God created us for *us*, not for himself. Everything God tells us to do or not to do is for *our* sake and benefit, not his.

> Everything God tells us to do or not to do is for *our* sake and benefit, not his.

Therefore, again as the Apostle John says, the motivation is love, not fear:

> There is no fear in love. Instead, perfect love drives fear away. Fear has to do with being punished. The one who fears does not have perfect love.
>
> (1 John 4:15–18)

In other words, knowing of God's incredible love and plan for us should drive away any fear that we may have of following God or of doing things his way. It should, in fact, send us running to him, no longer wanting to do things our way but wanting to fully embrace God's love and care.

Our goal as parents should be to help our children know how much God loves them and how much good he wants to do for them, so that they can trust him with every part and every moment of their lives. They should know that they can trust that every decision they make according to his principles and his direction is in the long run the best possible decision they could make; reliance on God takes them on the path to becoming the best possible "them" they can be and to living the best life they can live.

To come back to a point made at the beginning of this chapter: yes, God sees everything that your children do. But he sees it not from up in the sky but from right there with them. And if they're doing something wrong, he doesn't get mad and put demerit marks on heaven's eternal blackboard. Your children should feel that they can talk to God, that he understands how they feel and why they're doing what they're doing, that he wants to and will help them. They shouldn't feel that they need to run and hide from him. When they're in trouble is when they need God's love and help most, and that's when they need to know that God wants not to punish them but to *help* them.

How can I explain to my children what God's character is like?

I WANTED TO BRING GOD FOR SHOW AND TELL, BUT I COULDN'T. SO I THOUGHT OF THE NEXT CLOSEST THING: OUR TEACHER, MRS. BRUMMEL. SHE TEACHES US, LETS US DO FUN THINGS, AND ...AHEM...SHE ALWAYS GIVES US GREAT MARKS ON THESE KINDS OF PRESENTATIONS.

In some ways, God is very different from us. He's *God*, and he's awesome. He's the creator, and we're creatures. But that doesn't mean that we should talk about God in terms of his being so big and mysterious that we can't possibly understand who he is and what he's like. Even the unique and awesome things about God can be put in simple terms for children to understand.

Yet in many ways God is similar to us, and that's what we should focus on first when we talk to our kids about God. He made us "in his image." People have debated a lot about exactly what that phrase means, but one thing is for sure: everything good that God created as part of who we are is part of who God is, even though he's not limited to or by any of these things.

With God revealing himself as being so similar to us in so many ways, we should be able to avoid talking about God as unknowable and completely mysterious. It's through these similarities that our kids can easily begin to understand who God is and what he's like, and to feel more comfortable with him and relate to him better. Here are some of the ways in which God has shown himself to be similar to us (or rather, ways in which we're similar to God):

- He's creative: he loves to design and make new things.
- He's love: he enjoys giving and caring for others.
- He has emotions: he feels, and he expresses the way he feels.
- He has a sense of humor: he laughs and has fun.
- He loves beauty: music and art and nature.
- He loves being in relationships: he wants to know and be with us, as his children and his friends.
- He loves wisdom: understanding and knowledge.
- He talks and thinks: he plans and builds, and he pursues goals, enjoying work time and rest time in the process.

It's important that our children have an accurate understanding of God's character for three solid reasons. First, in order for them to trust God and develop a relationship with him, they need to know what he's like and what they can expect of him. Second, God created everything, including life itself, in harmony with his character, so understanding his character is essential to a successful life. And third, understanding God's character gives children a picture of what their own character should look like.

Here are four foundational descriptions of God's character, from the Bible, that you can use to help your children better understand who God is.

God Is the Inventor and Creator of Life

I've already talked a lot about learning, growing, responsibility, and other serious things. Although our kids' spiritual life
isn't something we should take lightly, we can get so wrapped
up in the seriousness of it all that we end up painting God as
a sour-faced old schoolmarm who demands that we get serious, sit quietly, and do only what we're told to do. That's why
this first aspect of God's character is so critically important
and why I put it first.

God invented
        beauty
        joy
            happiness
            humor
                laughter
                    applause
                        sunshine
                            entertainment
                        fun
                            health
                                nature
                                    sports
                                    love
                                        friendship
                                        families
                                            conversation
                                            art
                                                drama
                                                music
                                                food
                                                    animals
                                                    and even hugs.

It's important that we talk about God in relation to the
good things in life, that we talk about him during the *good*

times and not just when we need to lecture about right and wrong or struggle with someone's death or sickness or explain why some disaster took place. Our children would quickly get tired of our company if all we did was teach and correct, even if we did it gently. They'd also want to be somewhere else, *anywhere* else, if we were always mad, upset, or negative.

It's the same with God. We can't get away with talking about God only in dour terms and in dour times and still expect our children to be excited about developing a relationship with him. Instead, we should focus on seeing him as the inventor behind life's joys, the one who's throwing the party, not the one who's scolding everyone and sending them home. "God . . . richly provides us with everything to enjoy" (1 Timothy 6:17).

God is there with us and for us, and he gives us all the good things listed above to enjoy—and a whole lot of others that aren't mentioned.

God Is Good

God is good, and therefore what he does is good. Our children should understand that God created them for good things. His desire is to be good to our children, to give them good things, and to teach them and help them so that they can have a good life. God isn't a mean and angry God; he's good, kind, and loving, and he acts accordingly.

> The Lord God is like the sun that gives us light.
> He is like a shield that keeps us safe.
> The Lord blesses us with favor and honor.
> He doesn't hold back anything good from those whose lives
>   are without blame.
>
> (PSALM 84:11)

> Lord, you are good. You are forgiving.
> You are full of love for all who call out to you.
>
> (PSALM 86:5)

You are good, and what you do is good.

(PSALM 119:68)

Even though you [people] are evil, you know how to give good gifts to your children. How much more will your Father who is in heaven give good gifts to those who ask him!

(MATTHEW 7:11)

Every good and perfect gift is from God. It comes down from the Father. He created the heavenly lights. He does not change like shadows that move.

(JAMES 1:17)

We know that in all things God works for the good of those who love him. He appointed them to be saved in keeping with his purpose.

(ROMANS 8:28)

God is good to us—and our children need to be good to others. Being good to others and doing good are keys to a successful, happy life. When our children's intent is to do good to others, people see it in their lives and respect them, trust them, and want to be with them. When they do good to others, they feel great about themselves, and their confidence and self-image improve. They gain a feeling of fulfillment; they become more accepted, appreciated, and loved as members of our society; and others want to, and begin to, do good for them. In other words, God rewards them—and us—for doing good to others. "Good" makes life work.

Let us not become tired of doing good. At the right time we will gather a crop if we don't give up. So when we can do good to everyone, let us do it.

(GALATIANS 6:9–10)

Remind God's people to obey rulers and authorities. Remind them to be ready to do what is good. Tell them not to speak evil things against anyone. Remind them to live in peace. They must consider the needs of others. They must be kind and gentle toward all people.

(TITUS 3:1–2)

Then those who have trusted in God will be careful to commit themselves to doing what is good.

(TITUS 3:8)

Don't forget to do good. Don't forget to share with others. God is pleased with those kinds of offerings.

(HEBREWS 13:16)

God Understands

God understands. He will always listen, understand, and respond to our children, no matter what happens in their lives. God is always right there for them. He understands everything they feel and go through, and he's always ready to encourage them to go forward, to give them wisdom, and to help them out. God is on their side.

The New Testament book of Hebrews tells us that Jesus is fully sympathetic, understanding even the toughest things we go through because he also went through them. Sometimes we forget that Jesus was once a child and then a teenager. (The Bible even records a time when his parents didn't understand him!) Jesus had to be obedient to his parents, go to school, do chores, and grow up in a community of friends, neighbors, and family. The single incident from Jesus' childhood included in the Bible—something that happened when he was twelve years old—seems to have been recorded to show us that Jesus had to grow up just like everyone else.

Our children can take comfort in the fact that when they pray and talk to God, they have someone listening who's on their side, who completely understands how they feel and what they're going through, and who's ready to help.

We have a high priest [Jesus] who can feel it when we are weak and hurting. We have a high priest who has been tempted in every way, just as we are. But he did not sin. So let us boldly approach the throne of grace. Then we will receive mercy. We will find grace to help us when we need it.

(HEBREWS 4:15–16)

Whatever our troubles are, however besieged we feel, God can and will help.

What should we say then? Since God is on our side, who can be against us?

(ROMANS 8:31)

God understands us, and our children need to be taught likewise to be understanding of others, because when they love, accept, and forgive others, always trying to understand and to give them the benefit of the doubt, they become the kind of people that others feel good about and want to be with. When people know that our children don't gossip, judge, or say negative things about others, those people can be confident that our kids won't judge *them* either. When our children learn to be compassionate and understanding of others, many doors in life will be opened to them. Everyone on this planet wants to be loved, understood, and thought well of. When our children know how to imitate their Father with this character trait, and they imitate him from the heart, many of the people they encounter will want to be their friend, will accept them into their group or community, and will hire them, promote them, and honor and respect them. Life works by understanding and compassion.

But love your enemies. Do good to them. Lend to them without expecting to get anything back. Then you will receive a lot in return. And you will be children of the Most High God. He is kind to people who are evil and are not thankful. So have mercy, just as your Father has mercy.

If you do not judge others, then you will not be judged. If you do not find others guilty, then you will not be found guilty. Forgive, and you will be forgiven. Give, and it will be given to you.

(LUKE 6:35–38)

Those who have no sense make fun of their neighbors.
But those who have understanding control their tongues.
Those who talk about others tell secrets.
But those who can be trusted keep things to themselves.

(PROVERBS 11:12–13)

God Is Trustworthy and Faithful

When our children turn to God as their Father and begin to rely on his working in and with them, and in their lives, they need to know that he's trustworthy and faithful.

It's impossible to trust someone when you know nothing of his or her character, concern for you, or ability to deliver. To trust someone means that you know, without even having to think about it, that because of his or her character and love for you, that person will always act with your best interests in mind. You know that the person in question is *trustworthy*. It also means having the confidence that the person you trust is not only *able* to do what you're trusting him or her to do but *will* do it—because that person is *faithful*.

Our children, then, need to know that God loves them and is *trustworthy;* they can trust him with their lives, knowing that his way is the best way and will make their lives work better. They also need to know that he's *faithful;* they can put their faith in him and rely on him, day by day, to do what he says he'll do for them as their Father: care for them, provide for them, teach them, direct and encourage them, help them to grow, and so forth.

What the Lord says is right and true.
He is faithful in everything he does.

(PSALM 33:4)

The Lord is faithful and will keep all his promises.
He is loving toward everything he has made.

(PSALM 145:13)

Let us hold firmly to the hope we claim to have. The One
who promised is faithful.

(HEBREWS 10:23)

He is faithful and right in everything he does.
All his rules can be trusted.

(PSALM 111:7)

Lord, those who know you will trust in you.
You have never deserted those who look to you.

(PSALM 9:10)

May the God who gives hope fill you with great joy. May you
have perfect peace as you trust in him. May the power of the
Holy Spirit fill you with hope.

(ROMANS 15:13)

Our children also need to be trustworthy and faithful
themselves. These two characteristics are foundational for
establishing relationships and making them grow. Trustworth-
iness and faithfulness are necessary if your children are going
to be successful in relationships with friends and family, in
marriage, and in their careers and communities. If people
can trust them to do what's best for others and can put their
faith in their ability to perform and to keep their word, they'll
prosper in their relationships. And since good relationships
are the key to success in every area of human existence,

they'll succeed in life. Furthermore, if they're trustworthy and faithful in their relationship with God, God will be able to trust them with more responsibilities and blessings in this life. Life works when we're faithful and trustworthy.

> Don't let love and truth ever leave you.
> Tie them around your neck.
> Write them on the tablet of your heart.
> Then you will find favor and a good name
> in the eyes of God and people.
>
> (PROVERBS 3:3–4)

> Lord, to those who are faithful you show that you are faithful.
> To those who are without blame you show that you are without blame.
>
> (PSALM 18:25)

> Friends love at all times.
> They are there to help when trouble comes.
>
> (PROVERBS 17:17)

> Whoever can be trusted with very little can also be trusted with much, and whoever is dishonest with very little will also be dishonest with much.
>
> (LUKE 16:10, NIV)

You can see now why correctly teaching our children about God's character is vital if we want them to have a successful life!

An additional resource for helping your children understand the character of God is a series of seven books by C. S. Lewis known as the Chronicles of Narnia. This series includes *The Lion, the Witch, and the Wardrobe; The Voyage of the Dawn Treader;* and *Prince Caspian.* The main character in the series is Aslan, the great lion who created the country Narnia as well as our world. You can point out to your children how Aslan represents the marvelous character of God in his majesty and his playfulness, his compassion and his power. Apart from the deeper meaning of the character of Aslan, the books are also delightful stories for kids (of all ages).

How can I answer my children's questions about such things as God's omnipotence and the Trinity?

When talking to our kids about how God is *different* from us, we need to be careful not to make our children feel far away from God by explaining these differences in a way that makes it impossible for them to relate to or comprehend. Instead, we can focus on how God's differences benefit us and make him all the more wonderful, powerful, and available as a loving Father.

It's important to cover three very basic facts about God to begin with: first, God has no beginning and no end; he has always existed and always will. Second, God created everything that exists, and nothing that exists came into existence apart from him. Third, there's no other God; he's the only one.

We all, at some point in our lives, muse over and try to make sense of these three facts about God and about other ways in which God differs from us. Our thoughts seem to trip over themselves as we wrestle with understanding these concepts.

It's certainly reasonable for our minds to spin a bit when thinking of these things. But it's *not* reasonable to conclude that because we have trouble comprehending or proving them, God can't be real. That would be like our making something out of clay, only to have the thing we made argue that it's impossible for us to exist because we weren't baked in a kiln!

Let's look now at some of the other ways God differs from us.

God Is Everywhere (He Is Omnipresent)

God doesn't have a physical, in-one-place-only body. He's spirit, and he's present everywhere all the time. But if you leave your children with only that description, they'll start thinking of God as air or as a formless ghost. It can be very hard for children to relate to a Heavenly Father who has no substance and is in no particular place.

So how can we help them understand? First of all, just because God is spirit doesn't mean that he can't be in a specific place at a particular time or that he has no substance. Angels are spirit too, but the Bible describes them as having form and substance. But while angels can be in only one place at a time, God is described in the Bible as being able to simultaneously be in one spot and be everywhere. Yet he's not depicted like air and without substance: the Bible talks many times about God's throne and throne room, allowing us to picture him with substance and in one spot. God represented himself visibly to the Israelites in a cloud on many different occasions, again demonstrating his willingness to be understood in a more concrete manner. And the Genesis account talks about God walking in the Garden of Eden with Adam and Eve.

One way to help your children understand this concept is to use the analogy of an aquarium. Though very limited, the analogy is effective for this purpose. The fish see the aquarium as a big place—as their entire world. It's impossible for them to see more than one small part of it at a time. However, your children can look at the aquarium and see all of the fish and their entire world all at once. Your children still have substance; it's just that both their field of vision and their ability to gather information are far greater than those of the fish.

> The fact that God can be everywhere at the same time means that he can give each one of us his personal love and attention and be with us always.

While explaining this to our children, we can use the opportunity to reinforce the benefits of putting our lives in God's hands. The fact that God can be everywhere at the same time means that he can give each one of us his personal love and attention and be with us always. It's like having a personal teacher or coach as opposed to sharing one teacher or coach with thirty other kids. It means that when you want to talk to God, you never get a busy signal.

God Can Do Anything (He Is Omnipotent)

With all the big-screen superheroes in our culture today, the concept of omnipotence isn't hard for children to grasp. However, we need to help them know that in God's case the power is absolutely true and real. We also need to help them understand the difference between God and the superheroes: God's power isn't the power of fists and guns; it's the power of love, compassion, and forgiveness.

Simply put, nothing is impossible for God. He can do anything and everything, and he's more than willing to use his ability to help, because he's love. The Bible says that nothing is impossible to the person who believes and trusts God. We should teach our children that no matter what happens in life or what they come up against, they can rely on the One who can do anything to help them overcome, solve, or get through the problem.

God Knows Everything (He Is Omniscient)

God knows everything there is to know. This includes all information that exists anywhere, as well as the knowledge of everything that's ever happened anywhere, is currently happening, and will happen in the future. It can be tempting at times to use this information as a threatening reminder that our children should behave themselves. We need to resist that temptation, however. Instead, we should present God's omniscience to our children as an incredibly awesome benefit to life. If our kids are in need of understanding or knowledge about absolutely anything, they can go to God and ask for his wisdom and his guidance and his direction:

> If any of you need wisdom, ask God for it. He will give it to you. God gives freely to everyone. He doesn't find fault.
>
> (JAMES 1:5)

God knows everything there is to know. It can be tempting at times to use this information as a threatening reminder that our children should behave themselves. We need to resist that temptation.

Solomon, a great king mentioned in the Bible, sincerely and wholeheartedly asked God for wisdom. God didn't just say abracadabra and all of a sudden Solomon's brain was crammed with all manner of wisdom and knowledge. On the contrary, Solomon started on a journey when he began trusting God to teach him. He learned to pursue wisdom and knowledge with all his heart while being tuned in to the One who knows everything.

Sometimes we think that Solomon's wisdom was limited to knowing how to handle people and life situations properly. But the Bible and history record that Solomon, besides being a great king, was also a master builder, an expert in botany and zoology, and a master of finance, commerce, and international trade. He made

> There's a big difference between information and wisdom. We can get information from books and the Internet, but wisdom comes from God.

his country and his people so wealthy that silver became worthless and was piled up in the streets.

We should also make clear to our kids that there's a big difference between information and wisdom. We can get information from books and the Internet, but wisdom comes from God. Information is stuff that can be stored on hard disks and floppies. But all the information in the world can't help us live life the way God intended it. Wisdom, on the other hand, is knowing and being able to apply the principles that God gave us to function in harmony with the way he created life to work. Solomon himself tells us over and over in the Old Testament book of Proverbs that the key to life is wisdom and the key to wisdom is trusting the One who created and knows everything.

A great way to help our children understand the benefit of their Heavenly Father knowing everything is to tell them that they have, with them and on their side, the greatest teacher, coach, trainer, financial adviser, career counselor, family counselor, and overall life-planning expert possible.

There Is Only One God, but He Exists in Three Persons (The Trinity)

The New Testament clearly describes the Father as God, Jesus as God, and the Holy Spirit as God. But the Bible also says that there's only *one* God. This means that these three distinct persons are at the same time one.

For some children, this apparent contradiction isn't a problem at all. They simply accept that that's the way God is, and that's wonderful. But other kids try to understand it rationally. In talking with that second group, we have a choice: (1) we can try to explain the Trinity in accurate theological terms (assuming we can do that!), (2) we can try to avoid an explanation by telling them that "that's just the way God is" (which goes counter to everything else we're trying to do in helping our kids relate to God!), or (3) we can try to explain the Trinity in the simplest possible terms and help our children understand what that concept means in their lives.

Perhaps the easiest way to explain "one God, three persons" is this. We as human beings understand complete separation: each one of us can be in only one spot at one time, we know only what we've learned (and not what somebody else has learned), we can think only our own thoughts (and not somebody else's), and we all have different abilities. But what if our limitations suddenly disappeared? What if all of us could be everywhere at the same time instead of in only one spot? Then all of us would be everywhere! What if all of us suddenly knew everything? Then all of us would know everything and thus have exactly the same knowledge. And so on.

We can only imagine what it would be like, but in the case of God it is true. God the Father, God the Son, and God the Holy Spirit all can do anything, all know absolutely everything, and all are absolutely everywhere at the same time; so they're one in thought, knowledge, presence, power, and ability. Yet they're different. What is it that separates them? It's their unique persons, each with a separate task.

When Jesus was on the earth he was baptized in water by John the Baptist. The gospels tell us that when he came out of the water, the Holy Spirit came down on him like a dove, and God spoke from heaven (Luke 3:21–22). In this picture we see the Father, the Son, and the Holy Spirit all presented together, all working together, and yet each one completing a separate task.

Here's a simple way to explain the separate roles that God the Father, God the Son, and God the Holy Spirit have in our kids' lives.

- God is their Father; he's the one they're to pray to, trust, and develop a relationship with.
- Jesus is God's Son, and he died for us so that we could join God's family; he's our Savior and role model.
- The Holy Spirit helps us get to know God, learn from him, and grow as his children, and he directs and guides us into the life that God has designed for us.

God is greater than we can comprehend. But he's described himself thoroughly so that we can better relate to him and can understand that he's more than able to love us and take care of us individually and completely, as our Heavenly Father.

How can I help my children have a strong faith in God?

LOOK DAD! I CAN WALK ON WATER!

There are three practical things you can do to strengthen your children's belief in God:

- Help them see that their faith is reasonable.
- Help them see God working in their lives.
- Help them see God through what he's created.

Seeing That Their Faith Is Reasonable

We should never tell our children that having faith and believing in God is something that doesn't make sense, that flies in the face of reason. God created our intellect and our ability to reason, and he doesn't require us to check them at the door of faith.

Jesus appealed to people's intellect and reason repeatedly, even when it came to believing:

> Do not believe me unless I do what my Father does. But if I do it, even though you do not believe me, believe the miracles, that you may know and understand that the Father is in me, and I in the Father.
>
> (JOHN 10:37–38)

> After his suffering and death, he [Jesus] appeared to them. In many ways he proved that he was alive. He appeared to them over a period of 40 days. During that time he spoke about God's kingdom.
>
> (ACTS 1:3)

Similarly, the Apostles Paul and Peter used arguments of reason when trying to convince others to believe, including reminding them of Jesus' miracles, which many in the community either had seen or knew of, and using the testimony of the more than five hundred people who had seen Jesus after he rose from the dead.

Showing our children that their faith is reasonable also prepares them for the inevitable onslaught of conflicting information they'll receive from others. There are many good resources available that can assist you in this task, but I offer here a few simple facts that you can use in discussions with your children. Just knowing some of these basics will help your kids see that their faith is indeed reasonable.

Have your children imagine that your family is walking through the forest. There, beside the path, you see a beautiful gold pocket watch. You pick it up and say, "Wow! This is truly remarkable; this watch just came together all by itself over thousands of years

> Saying that the earth and all of creation came into existence without a creator is like saying that the Mona Lisa is the result of a paint spill or that the dictionary is the result of an explosion in a print shop.

through a remarkable string of chance happenings." As you try to convince your children of your conclusion, they'll try to convince you of how ridiculous you're being. Now help them see that they automatically assumed that the intricate design of the watch was a sure sign that it had been designed and put together by someone.

The odds of everything in creation coming together through a remarkable string of chance happenings are so astronomical that there are no computers big enough on this earth to calculate them. One thing is for sure: it's many, many times more likely that the pocket watch came together by itself. Saying that the earth and all of creation came into existence without a creator is like saying that the Mona Lisa is the result of a paint spill or that the dictionary is the result of an explosion in a print shop.

The odds of all the components that make up a single-cell creature coming together by themselves in just the right way to form life have been calculated to range from 1 in 10^{60} to 1 in $10^{40,000}$. (That's a 1 with 40,000 zeros after it!) Even the lowest odds of 1 in 10^{60} are insurmountable. And those are the odds for a *single*-cell life form! Not only is a human being made of millions of cells—which compounds the odds astronomically—but each cell in our bodies must work in absolute harmony with every other cell. (If just one cell is out of place, our bodies may not function properly. A single cancerous cell, for example, can destroy life.) Add the incredible complexity required for the proper functioning of the body, and the enormous number of cells in the body, to the odds of even a single cell coming together by chance—and the odds are simply beyond calculation.

The picture of the origin of humanity that's usually presented in popular books about evolution involves a series of life forms beginning with a single cell in the ocean. That single-cell creature evolves, via fish that crawl up on shore, to apes and then to humans in a nice, continuous parade. But there are two things missing in this picture: time and transitions.

The earth, according to evolutionists, is four billion years old. That's a long time by our standards, but as a time frame for evolution from inert matter to human beings, it's wholly inadequate. Some scientists realize this. One solution, proposed by respected scientists, involves the assumption that life forms evolved on another planet where there *was* enough time, and that their seeds were transported to earth on meteorites and comets (I'm not making this up!).[1] But this doesn't solve the problem; it simply extends the boundaries and finds more time elsewhere—with no additional proof.

The second thing that's missing is transitions: the so-called missing links. If all life evolved from simple molecules to human beings, one would expect to find transitions between, say, reptiles and birds and between apes and humans. These transitional forms haven't been found. One solution, proposed by Stephen Jay Gould, is the theory of *punctuated equilibrium*. He argues that species existed for hundreds of millions of years in equilibrium—that is, without any significant change—punctuated by brief periods of only a few million years each during which mutations and changes happened at an extremely rapid rate. The result, he claims, is an abundance of fossils from the long periods of equilibrium and (of necessity) very few from the short periods of change. It's a neat solution, but it begs the question. It assumes that the fossil record of change is there, even though we haven't found it yet. But without the fossil record to prove that transitional forms existed, that assumption is just that—an assumption.

But what about the links that have been found between apes and humans? Many of the most promising finds have turned out to be either a hoax (as with Piltdown Man, *Eoanthropus*, which was later identified as a human skullcap buried next to the lower jaw of an orangutan) or a simple case of misidentification. For example, Nebraska Man

---

[1] Fred Hoyle and N. C. Wikramasinghe, *Evolution From Space: A Theory of Cosmic Creation* (New York: Simon and Schuster, 1981).

(Hesperopithecus) was created from a single tooth that was eventually recognized as belonging to an extinct pig; SW Colorado Man was also built from a single tooth—one that turned out to have belonged to an extinct horse; and Java Man, hailed as a key evolutionary link, was later found to be the fossilized remains of a large, ground-walking gibbon. Heidelberg Man, reconstructed from a jawbone, is still considered a missing link, yet fully human natives of New Caledonia today have the same jawbone. In other words, the link is still missing.

So what do we mean by a "reasonable faith"? Having such a faith doesn't mean that we can or have to prove to everybody else's satisfaction that God exists or that everything we believe about God is true. Rather, a reasonable faith is simply a faith that doesn't go against reason. Here's one way you can illustrate this point to your kids.

There are extremely small, short-lived, subatomic particles that no one has ever seen. They were believed to exist before anyone had ever observed evidence of them, because everything else known about particles indicated that they *should* be there. Later they were shown to exist by trails they left behind in highly sensitive equipment. Was it reasonable to believe, before they had been proven to exist, that these particles were there and could be found? Of course. Is it reasonable to believe that these particles really exist even though no one has ever *seen* one? Of course. The *effect* they have on their surroundings,

> Having a "reasonable faith" doesn't mean that we can or have to prove to everybody else's satisfaction that God exists or that everything we believe about God is true. Rather, a reasonable faith is a faith that doesn't go against reason.

> Either God stands at the beginning of time or he doesn't. The choice, either way, is a matter of faith. And if—by faith—you accept that God *wasn't* there, then you have to work hard to find alternative explanations that make sense.

which *can* be observed, is enough to make scientists accept that they exist.

The odd thing is that the same logic isn't applied when we talk about the origin of the universe and of life. No one can go back and *prove* what happened at the beginning of time—neither the people who believe that God created the universe and life, nor the people who believe that either there is no God or that God had nothing to do with whatever happened to bring about time, space, matter, and life.

Yet either God stands at the beginning of time or he doesn't. The choice, either way, is a matter of faith. And if—by faith—you accept that God *wasn't* there, then you have to work hard to find alternative explanations that make sense.

It's important to help our kids understand that we *all* believe things we can't prove—though some are more reasonable than others. But we don't have to be put on the defensive because we have faith in God. Based on the available evidence and the effects we can see, faith in God seems a whole lot more reasonable than any of the alternatives.

If you're interested in more information that will help you show your children that their faith is reasonable, check the following Web site: *lightwavepublishing.com.*

Seeing God Working in Their Lives

The second way in which we can strengthen our children's faith in God is to help them experience God, or see him at work in their lives. A Gallup youth survey reported that 95 percent of teens said that they believe in God or a universal Spirit, 93 percent said that they believe that God loves them, but only 29 percent said that they've personally experienced the presence of God.[2]

---

[2]*Youthviews: The Newsletter of the Gallup Youth Survey* (Princeton, N.J.: George H. Gallup International Institute), vol. 3, no. 8 (Apr. 1996).

It's great that our kids believe in God and that they believe he loves them, but God wants to *demonstrate* that love in their lives. Our children should be able to see the results and the effects of God's love and his Fathering. We would think it unreasonable if someone continually told us that he or she loved us but never did anything about it. Contrary to the popular saying, it's *not* the thought that counts. Without corresponding action, there's no way to demonstrate the existence of the thought. The Bible teaches us that we must demonstrate our faith by showing our love for our fellow humans. God wants to do the same thing for us.

Often we distance ourselves from God, his active participation in our lives, and his very real answers to prayer by thinking either that our concerns are too small to bother him with or that we can handle things ourselves. But God wants to demonstrate his love in very real and wonderful ways. Nothing is too small or unimportant to bring to his attention. He wants us to talk with him and trust him about *everything*, big and small:

> Don't worry about anything. Instead, tell God about everything. Ask and pray. Give thanks to him. Then God's peace will watch over your hearts and your minds because you belong to Christ Jesus.
>
> (PHILIPPIANS 4:6–7)

> My God will meet all your needs. He will meet them in keeping with his wonderful riches that come to you because you belong to Christ Jesus.
>
> (PHILIPPIANS 4:19)

> God did not spare his own Son. He gave him up for us all. Then won't he also freely give us everything else?
>
> (ROMANS 8:32)

The author of the biblical book of Hebrews said,

> Without faith it isn't possible to please God. Those who come to God must believe that he exists. And they must believe that he rewards those who look to him.
>
> (HEBREWS 11:6)

It's important to believe that God exists, but God wants us to move on from there and believe that he rewards us as we look to him as our Father. God insists that we can trust him and should believe that he'll be incredibly good to us. We need to help our children understand who God is and make sure that they're confident that he'll express his love and care not just in theory but in reality, in the mundane details of their lives. God is not an absentee Father.

Talking to our children about all of the things that God has said he is willing to do in their lives, as their Father, is a necessary foundation. Then, as life's stage provides the opportunities, we should gently remind them and guide them—with all their needs, questions, and desires—toward God and his love. As God responds to their simple faith—sometimes boldly, sometimes subtly—we can help them see God in his answers.

At the heart of our children's simple faith is prayer—the essence of their relationship with God. Prayer isn't a science, nor does it work like the shopping channel. Certainly the things they pray for and about shouldn't read like a list for Saint Nick. Their prayers should include petitions for others, for wisdom, and for growth. We need to teach our children to trust that God will always hear them and do what's best for them with regard to the things they talk with him about in prayer.

When we encourage our children to trust God and talk with him about anything and everything, his answers and the demonstration of his love will begin to show up in many different forms.

When we encourage our children to trust God and talk with him about anything and everything, his answers and the demonstration of his love will begin to show up in many different forms—in direct, obvious answers to prayer, in situations that work out better than we could have expected them to, and in many other ways that our children would miss if we weren't there pointing to God's love at work in their lives. Talk to your children about the times that you've seen God answer your prayers. These stories will be a great inspiration to your children and will motivate them to want to make a collection of similar stories in their own lives. (We'll talk in more detail about teaching our children about prayer and how to pray in a later chapter.) Being a Christian doesn't mean simply that we believe in God; it also means that we *experience* God and his love.

Another way in which we can help our children experience God is to assist them to see the results of doing things God's way and following his principles. When your children choose right over wrong, take the time to not only praise them for their wisdom but also point out the immediate and long-term benefits of their actions. The more evidence they see that doing things God's way *works,* the stronger their faith and their resolve to follow God will become.

Seeing God Through What He Has Created

A third way to strengthen our children's faith in God is to help them see his power and his character in what he's created. As the Apostle Paul says,

> Ever since the world was created it has been possible to see the qualities of God that are not seen. I'm talking about his eternal power and about the fact that he is God. Those things can be seen in what he has made.
>
> (ROMANS 1:20)

The awesomeness of human beings is an incredible testimony to God's power and love. Whenever you see a news article or television show about medical discoveries and the phenomenal inner workings of the human body, or when your children learn about such things at school, take the opportunity to point out God's incredible design and the love he demonstrated in making us so wonderful and so complete.

Next time you're looking out at the stars, or your children are learning about the incredible vastness of our universe, take the opportunity to help your children see how unlimited and powerful God is.

Point out to your children how everything in creation works in perfect harmony and balance: the way the food chain works; how our atmosphere is perfect for sustaining life; how the atmosphere is maintained by the amazing cooperation of different systems we often take for granted; how each creature that God has made, from bacteria to whales, has a special role in maintaining the balance of life on earth. All of this demonstrates God's loving character through his care for us and for all of creation.

The intricacy of detail that supports and undergirds all of creation—molecules, atoms, protons, neutrons, electrons, quarks, and the incredible principles and laws that govern the microscopic domain—show that God is diligent and caring, concerned with every detail, finding nothing too small for his concern.

And when your kids watch a butterfly just because it's beautiful, or spend time with a playing kitten just because it's funny, or sit by the gutter in the rain just because they're intrigued by the ever-changing patterns in the water, we can help them see God in the aesthetic beauty of everyday life.

We're surrounded by the best tools available to help strengthen our children's faith in God. When we show our kids that what they believe is reasonable, their faith is anchored; when we help them experience God's love, their faith is made real and practical; and when we help them see God's power and character in his creation, their faith is inspired.

2.

The Bible

~~~~~~

A. How can I show my children that the Bible is trustworthy?

B. What kind of Bible or Bible storybook should I use with my children?

C. How can I tell my kids in a simple way what the Bible is all about?

D. What can I do to help my kids get a handle on how all the pieces of the Bible fit together?

E. What are some practical tips for reading the Bible to or with my kids?

F. How can I help my kids read through the Bible?

G. Is there value in having my kids memorize verses from the Bible?

~~~~~~

How can I show my children that the Bible is trustworthy?

An ABC News poll conducted in March 1997 asked the question, "Which one of these statements comes closest to describing your feelings about the Bible?"

a. The Bible is the actual Word of God to be taken literally, word for word.
b. The Bible is the inspired Word of God; not everything should be taken word for word.
c. The Bible is an ancient book of fables, legends, history, and mere perceptions recorded by man.

Of those polled, 42 percent answered (a), another 43 percent answered (b), and only 12 percent answered (c), while 3 percent offered no opinion. In short, 85 percent of us believe that the Bible is God's book.

Okay, so most of us believe that the Bible is God's book. But for a lot of people it's like being computer-illiterate and having a state-of-the-art computer with all the bells, whistles, and peripherals on the shelf. It's lovely, and undoubtedly very valuable, but what in the world do you *do* with it?

The parallel breaks down, of course, because our kids *would* know what to do with the computer. But when it comes to the Bible, they need help. In this section I want to give you some pointers about the Bible and how you can help your kids read and use it in daily life.

When you get to questions C and D, you may be tempted to skip the discussion because it doesn't seem very practical. Please don't. While those sections may not read like a John Grisham page-turner, in the long run the information they contain will turn out to be of immense practical benefit.

Elsewhere I've referred to the Bible as "God's instruction manual for life." But for many adults and older children, that description raises some questions.

The Bible was written by more than forty people from varied walks of life, from fishermen to doctors, from kings to outcasts. These people lived on three continents, wrote in three languages, and (since the whole process of writing the Bible took over fifteen hundred years) lived in a variety of cultures.

With a group of authors like that—people who wrote several millennia ago and had completely different backgrounds, professions, financial statuses, and cultural backgrounds— how can we possibly consider the Bible a guide for life *today?*

Several objections are often raised by skeptics today as proof that thinking people shouldn't put their trust in the Bible as God's guide to life. I want to briefly address those objections so that we as parents can feel confident when teaching our children from the Bible and can pass that confidence on to them.

- How can a book of which the most recent parts were written almost two thousand years ago be relevant and help my kids live in the twenty-first century?

- Since the Bible was copied by fallible human hands over and over again until the invention of the printing press five hundred years ago, how do we know that its text hasn't been hopelessly corrupted and changed?
- Since people several thousands of years ago weren't nearly as advanced as we are, can we trust that they knew what they were talking about?
- The Bible is a beautiful book, but how do we know that it's God's message to us?

Let's look at each of these objections in turn.

How Can an Ancient Book Give Guidance for the Twenty-first Century?

When Hollywood releases a movie about an event or figure set in the past, whether fictional or not, we as an audience can enjoy it as much as we do a film that's set in our own time. If it's a good movie, we forget that it's about the past; it's simply a story about people we identify with, and it's about life. The dated costumes and other trappings of a bygone era don't make the story distant from us, because below the surface people are no different today than they were thou-

> The principles that are taught in the Bible still apply today. All that's changed is the setting and the props.

sands of years ago, and the principles that govern relationships and life haven't changed.

We often hear that the Bible is irrelevant to our lives today because the issues and problems people faced were different when the Bible was written. But this objection makes little sense. Yes, the setting *was* different, and certainly it was less advanced technologically, but the core issues people dealt with were the same. Take finances, for example. Our currency is different from that of biblical times, and how and where we save and invest our money has drastically changed, as have the ways financial transactions take place. But the *principles* that are taught in the Bible about financial issues, such as having a solid work ethic, practicing integrity, saving, being generous, adopting fair business practices, avoiding get-rich-quick schemes, and spending frugally, still apply today. All that's changed is the setting and the props.

The Bible is completely relevant and useful today for teaching our children about God and life. Not only can God's principles be applied in any cultural setting, they can also be used as a yardstick for discerning where our culture has run off track. We need to help our children understand that God's principles don't limit cultural expression. Rather, God's principles undergird and support the enormous variety and range of cultures we see around us. Therefore, we should never use our culture as an excuse to redefine God's principles. Instead, we should use God's principles as the foundation and guide for evaluating and redefining our culture.

Hasn't the Text of the Bible Been Hopelessly Corrupted Over the Centuries?

If we accept that the Bible is relevant for today, we're still faced with the objection that fallible human scribes, in the process of copying the biblical message by hand over and over again for hundreds (and in the case of some portions, thousands) of years until printing was invented, corrupted the text. Yet the facts show otherwise.

The Bible is by far the best-preserved ancient manuscript in existence. We have over five thousand ancient handwritten copies (or parts of copies) of the New Testament and tens of thousands of pieces of copies of the Old Testament! Scholars who've compared the copies or pieces of copies from different time periods with what we have today have found that the copying was done accurately; differences are few, and none affects the substance of the Bible.

Until 1947, the oldest piece of the Old Testament we had dated from one hundred years after Jesus lived on earth. Then a shepherd boy in Israel found clay jars hidden in a cave above the Dead Sea. Those jars contained what are now known as the Dead Sea Scrolls. Among them was a scroll of the book of Isaiah that had been copied two hundred years before Jesus lived. That manuscript is almost exactly the same as what we read in our Bibles today.

The following quote is from the cover article of the December 18, 1995, issue of *TIME* magazine—an article titled "Is the Bible Fact or Fiction?"

> In 1979 Israeli archaeologist Gabriel Barkay found two tiny silver scrolls inside a Jerusalem tomb. They were dated to around 600 B.C., shortly before the destruction of Solomon's Temple and the Israelites' exile in Babylon. When scientists carefully unrolled the scrolls at the Israel Museum, they found a benediction from the Book of Numbers etched into their surface. The discovery made it clear that parts of the Old Testament were being copied long before some skeptics had believed they were even written.

We also have a manuscript (known as the *Codex Sinaiticus*) containing almost all of the New Testament that dates from about A.D. 350, only three hundred years after the last book of the New Testament was written, as well as a manuscript that may be slightly older and contains nearly the entire Bible (the *Codex Vaticanus*, A.D. 325–350). The oldest fragment of the New Testament that we have today is a piece of papyrus on which are recorded a few verses of the gospel of John, copied no more than seventy and perhaps as few as twenty years after John first wrote them!

The next-best-substantiated ancient document, in terms of how many hand-written copies (or portions of copies) exist today and how soon after the original they were copied, is Homer's *Iliad*. There are currently only 643 known copies of the *Iliad,* and the oldest is one made five hundred years after the original is believed to have been written.

If we believe that the Bible is God's Word, then we must believe that the same God who loved us enough to inspire it was able to deliver it to us in the form he intended it to be in. After all, if you were going to leave a very important message for your children, you'd make sure not only that you wrote it clearly enough that your instructions would be understood but also that you put it where it would be safe from damage so that they'd be sure to see it. That's exactly what God did: the Bible is the best-preserved, best-substantiated ancient book in existence today!

The Bible Is Said to Be Full of Errors, So How Can We Possibly Trust It?

Even if we accept that the Bible is relevant today and was transmitted with great accuracy, that doesn't help a whole lot if the original writings were full of errors, as some scholars would have us believe.

For centuries, people didn't worry too much about the fact that many of the people and places mentioned in the Bible were unknown and weren't mentioned in any other ancient writings. Then, in the nineteenth century, some scholars decided to use these references to otherwise unknown people and places as proof that the Bible writers simply made up stories and invented people and places as they went along. Furthermore, those scholars, operating on the assumption that writing hadn't been invented until well after Moses' time, concluded that the first six or seven books of the Bible had to have been written a long time after the events they recorded. The scholars ignored, of course, the possibility that the problem might be their own lack of knowledge of the past.

In the twentieth century, and especially in recent decades, the pendulum has swung back toward accepting the basic accuracy of the Bible. Archaeological discoveries, including ancient manuscripts that have come to light, show that the Bible rests on history rather than on fantasy. Over the years, one archaeological discovery after another has brought forward evidence confirming the historicity of characters and events mentioned in the Bible, of nations such as the Hittites, of cities such as Ur, and of various kings of Israel and Judah. And written records dating from many centuries before Moses have been unearthed!

I offer here just one specific example, found in the same *TIME* magazine article quoted earlier:

> In what may be the most important of these discoveries, a team of archaeologists uncovered a ninth century B.C. inscription at an ancient mound called Tel Dan, in the north of Israel, in 1993. Words carved into a chunk of basalt referred to the "House of David" and the "King of Israel." It is the first time the Jewish monarch's name has been found outside the Bible, and appears to prove he was more than mere legend.

There are many, many more such examples of evidence that support the essential historicity of the Bible. If you are interested in more information on the accuracy and preservation of the biblical text, you can turn to the following sources:

The Best of Josh McDowell: A Ready Defense, compiled by Bill Wilson (Nashville: Thomas Nelson, 1993).

The Bible Through the Ages (Pleasantville, N.Y.: The Reader's Digest Association, 1996).

Josh McDowell, *Evidence That Demands a Verdict* (San Bernardino: Here's Life Publishers, 1972, 1979).

But How Do We Know That the Bible Is the Word of God?

Even if we accept the first three points—that the Bible is relevant, accurate, and true—the most important question remains: How can we know that the Bible is God's Word for our lives today?

The first argument usually given is that the Bible is the Word of God because it *claims* to be—which isn't very convincing to people looking for some kind of logical proof, since logically this claim is valid only if the Bible really *is* the Word of God.

Frankly, there's no conclusive *logical* proof that the Bible was divinely inspired, just as there's no conclusive *logical* proof that God exists—or that I exist, or that the North Pole exists. But there's *practical* proof that in the long run is more convincing than any kind of proof based on logic. Perhaps the easiest way to get this proof across to kids is the following example:

Let's say you try to tell me that lions are beautiful but really dangerous, and I disagree with you. The lions I've seen in the zoo looked more like oversized kitties that yawn a lot than something to be scared of. The fact that I don't want to believe that lions are powerfully dangerous doesn't change the lions in any way, however. In fact, the best and only way to convince me if I refuse to accept the reasonableness of your argument is to simply let the lions loose while I visit the zoo. It may be the last thing I'll ever be convinced of in this life, but I'll finally have to agree with you that lions really *are* dangerous after all.

The same is true of the Bible. We can argue about the Bible till the cows come home, debating about what it is or isn't, but in the end our discussion doesn't change what the Bible *is*. The best way to prove the Bible to be the Word of God is simply to let it loose. Those who encounter it will find out that the Bible is the Word of God *because it changes lives*, as millions have experienced over the centuries.

> **There's no conclusive logical proof that the Bible was divinely inspired, just as there's no conclusive logical proof that God exists—or that I exist, or that the North Pole exists. But there's *practical* proof that in the long run is more convincing than any kind of proof based on logic.**

> The best way to prove the Bible to be the Word of God is simply to let it loose. Those who encounter it will find out that the Bible is the Word of God because it changes lives.

At least two Roman emperors, Decius and Diocletian, tried to destroy all of the Bibles in the empire. Despite their efforts, more copies of the Bible survived than of any other book from the days of the Roman empire. And today, in an era of million-copy best-sellers, the Bible has been read by more people, in more languages, than any other book. It was the first book to be printed on a printing press. Millions of Bibles or parts of Bibles are sold or given out every year around the world in hundreds of languages and dialects. The Bible is by far the world's all-time best-seller!

The Bible is not a religious handbook, given to the learned so that they could debate the theological impact of predestination on free will, or figure out how radical theism is to be reconciled with the idea of a Holy God, or to help them finally settle the question, If God can do anything, can he create a rock that's too big for him to move? If it *were* such a volume, we'd be wasting our time trying to get our kids to read it.

The Bible is simply given to us as an introduction to God and as a users' guide to life. It's our instruction manual—right down to introducing us to the manufacturer and letting us know how we can get in touch with him. Every newborn baby should be sent home from the hospital with a Bible. As the Bible says of itself,

> God has breathed life into all of Scripture. It is useful for teaching us what is true. It is useful for correcting our mistakes. It is useful for making our lives whole again. It is useful for training us to do what is right. By using Scripture, God's people can be completely prepared to do every good thing.
>
> (2 TIMOTHY 3:16–17)

Do not let this Book of the Law depart from your mouth; meditate on it day and night, so that you may be careful to do everything written in it. Then you will be prosperous and successful.

(JOSHUA 1:8)

The Bible is simply given to us as an introduction to God and as a users' guide to life.

What kind of Bible or Bible storybook should I use with my children?

Choosing a Bible or Bible storybook for our kids used to be relatively simple, since the choice was limited. Today it's a different story. We can choose from a wide variety of Bible storybooks for younger kids, most of them with colorful illustrations, as well as from many "regular" Bibles that contain the whole Bible text in language targeted at older children. It's well worth the time to investigate what's available, since not all Bible storybooks and "regular" Bibles for kids are of the same quality, and some may be better suited to some kids than to others. Here are some general tips:

- From the time children are old enough to be read to until the time they leave home, they'll probably go through four to six different Bibles. This is in part a practical necessity, since their reading skills, comprehension levels, and interests change, but it also helps kids see that learning about God is progressive (and that they are progressing). Graduating from one Bible to the next can be a real encouragement for our children, propelling them forward with newfound motivation.
- It's important that each of our children has his or her own Bible. That helps to show our kids how important the Bible is and emphasizes that the Bible always needs to be available as a book for learning and a practical guidebook for life. Of course, Bibles can be passed down to younger brothers and sisters as the older children grow out of them.
- When it's time to buy a new Bible, try to let your children choose their own. You can point out which Bibles or Bible storybooks are labeled for their age group, and they can make the final selection. This helps strengthen the ownership factor and increase the interest level.
- When your children are old enough to want a whole-text Bible, be sure to choose a translation that uses modern-day language so that your children will be able to understand what they're reading. You'll find the different Bibles labeled clearly as to which translation is used. Some modern-language translations are deliberately aimed at a lower reading level for kids. For example, the New International Reader's Version (NIrV) and the International Children's Version are both at a third-grade reading level, while the New Living Translation (NLT) is at a slightly higher level. If you're not familiar with the various modern translations, pick a few verses in different parts of the Bible and look them up in the various translations for comparison.

- Finally, look for whole-text children's and teen Bibles that contain additional materials that will help your children understand and apply what they read. Many Bibles for children and teens contain some or all of the following: a simple concordance, explanatory notes in the text, an introduction to each book of the Bible, maps of Bible lands, and cross-references to other places in the Bible that talk about the same topic. (See below, question E, for more about these helps.)

Here are a few hints for choosing a Bible storybook or a Bible by age group:

- *Preschoolers.* For this age group, a simply illustrated Bible storybook that covers the key Bible stories and has a small number of simple words per picture is appropriate.
- *Beginning Readers.* Several Bible storybooks have been created with simplified vocabularies at a reading level for the beginning reader. Your choice should be simply illustrated and contain more stories than a storybook for preschoolers. If you can find one that takes more than two pages to tell a story, your children will enjoy the stories more.
- *Grade-schoolers.* Look for a Bible storybook for this age group that contains more words and therefore more of the details of each story. Don't choose one, however, that has so many words and so few pictures that your child will give up. (The best balance of text and pictures will vary with the individual child, of course.) The illustrations for this level should be more detailed and interesting, but be careful to choose a book that has artwork that will appeal to your child. (Some children's Bible storybooks have been on the market for so long that the artwork is no longer current and exciting for today's kids.) Some Bible storybooks for this age group have a very simple Bible reference tool or index in the back, which is a plus.

- *Preteens and Early Teens.* This is the age group that usually wants to move away from a Bible storybook and go to a whole-text Bible. Allowing your children to help in the choice of the Bible at this age, if you haven't done so earlier, will greatly increase the effectiveness of the purchase. Be sure to steer them toward Bibles designed for preteens or teenagers, preferably with simple Bible reference tools in the back and helpful notes and features in and alongside the text.
- *Senior High Students.* When your children are in high school, they're beginning to think of themselves as grown-ups. This is a good time to move them to a Bible designed for adults. Again, allow them to make the choice, perhaps even to purchase the book on their own. Steer them, however, toward a good study Bible that has simple Bible reference tools and study notes.

In the last few decades, technology has created a whole range of new tools. Bibles and Bible storybooks are now available on CD-ROM, many with a variety of multimedia elements. Although these tools can be wonderful assistants in teaching our children the Bible, we should still have a hard copy available for them to read and carry, reinforcing its personal importance.

Another great tool, especially for younger kids, is video material that features animated Bible stories. Video Bible time shouldn't replace regular Bible study with our children, since part of what we're doing with our kids is helping them develop a lifelong habit of Bible reading. But videos can *augment* our teaching program: if used occasionally (perhaps once a week), they can be an exciting alternative to Bible reading, adding variety and fun to the process, enhancing kids' learning, and increasing their interest level.

How can I tell my kids in a simple way what the Bible is all about?

It's relatively easy to use a Bible storybook. Stories have been selected for us from the Bible, and we can simply read these stories to or with our kids. (Even if you're using a Bible storybook with your kids, the rest of this chapter can still be very helpful.) But when our kids are old enough to get a "regular" Bible—a Bible that has the whole text in it, from Genesis through Revelation—what are they supposed to do with it?

It would seem logical to simply start reading the Bible at the beginning and keep on reading until the end. But if you've ever tried to do that, you know what happens. The first book, Genesis, is incredibly engaging and full of wonderful stories—about creation, Noah's ark, Abraham, and so on. The next book, Exodus, begins with the great story of Moses and the pharaoh, but then come sections where we get bogged down in laws and detailed descriptions of the tabernacle. And when we discover that Leviticus is *all* laws, we quit and go back to reading just bits and pieces in the Bible—the stories we understand and are familiar with.

The problem is not that the stuff we get bogged down in doesn't make sense; rather, it's that without a larger context we don't know how to read it or what to do with it. It's like planning a trip by car from Toronto to San Diego with only a stack of city maps. You don't have a clue which towns you'll be traveling through until you look at a map of North America as a whole to give you the big picture. Then the maps of smaller areas such as provinces, states, and towns begin to make sense, because you understand them in a larger context.

In teaching any subject, it usually works best to start with an overview and gradually work our way down to the details. Then the details can be understood in terms of their wider context. Exactly the same thing is true of the Bible. The various stories of the Bible, as well as all the other pieces, such as laws and psalms, all fit into a Big Story—a single, coherent, wide-angle picture that serves as our roadmap through the Bible.

Most kids have heard Bible stories, but without the big picture, the Big Story of the Bible, they don't have a clue how the various stories are related to each other or in what order they did happen. Did Abraham come before or after Noah? Who came first, King David or Samson?

Knowing the stories is better than not knowing them, of course, even if the kids don't know how they fit together. But if we really want our kids to understand the Bible, we must help them understand these two relatively simple things:

> The various stories of the Bible, as well as all the other pieces, such as laws and psalms, all fit into a Big Story—a single, coherent, wide-angle picture that serves as our roadmap through the Bible.

- *The Big Story (or main storyline).* Once children grasp the outline of the Bible—the Big Story that weaves itself through both the Old and New Testaments, telling of God's plan for humanity and of how God has been working out that plan—they can fit the pieces into a larger context. The Big Story is what this section is about.
- *The structure of the Bible.* Children need to learn how the various books of the Bible fit into the Big Story so that they can find their way around in the Bible. We'll discuss that structure in the next section.

The Big Story

It began when God decided to make people that were in many ways like himself, people he could love. So he made the universe and everything in it, and then he made the first people, Adam and Eve, to be his children.

As their Father he loved them, and he wanted to have a loving relationship with them, their children, and all the people who came after them. He wanted to teach them and help them work together and use the amazing abilities and resources he had given them to build a phenomenal world. We can hardly imagine how marvelous his plan was and how awesome the future was for Adam and Eve and their offspring.

God gave Adam and Eve a beautiful garden to live in that provided everything they needed. God gave them only one rule: don't eat fruit from one tree, the "tree of the knowledge of good and evil," or you will die! But Satan, an important angel who had become God's enemy, disguised himself as a snake and lied to them. He told them that if they ate from that tree they wouldn't die at all; instead, they'd become like God, knowing good and evil.

God had made Adam and Eve and loved them. God knew that Adam and Eve needed to learn from him and trust his love so that he could give them the best life possible and help them become all they were intended to be. He wanted the very best for them, but he also wanted them to be able to learn and grow, to choose and create.

God allowed them to choose, but he warned them that if they chose their own path by disobeying him, they would separate themselves from him, from his plan, and from his blessings, all of which can be summed up in the word *life*. That separation from God and his wonderful gift of life can be summed up in the word *death*.

Adam and Eve made a choice. They took the fruit because they believed it would make them wise, but all it did was separate them from God and his loving direction. Satan had told a partial truth: they now knew good and evil, because they had done what was wrong, but they hadn't become like God. Instead, they were separated from true wisdom, which is always motivated by love. They had decided not to trust God's words about what was right and wrong. Instead, they decided for themselves what was right and wrong, good and evil.

When God created Adam and Eve, he said that everything was good. But after they ate of the fruit, the first thing Adam and Eve did was to decide for themselves that they were naked and that their nakedness was *not* good. By eating the fruit, man and woman had decided to leave God's way and find their own. They would now experience death instead of life. So God sent them out of the garden, away from what he had prepared for them, to let them find out that their own way wouldn't work.

As a result of Adam and Eve's choice and the separation from God that followed, everyone born after them would be born separated from God, wanting to find his or her own way—which is what the Bible uses the word *sin* for.

Humanity as a whole was now on a path of its own choice, and it didn't take long to become clear that the path led to death and destruction. Adam and Eve had children, and their first son, Cain, killed his brother, Abel. Soon the world was full of sinful people—that is, people who did as they pleased, with no regard for how God created things to work. People got worse and worse until they were downright evil.

God knew that he had to stop people from completely destroying each other and to somehow demonstrate that evil has grave consequences. He had a plan that would give people the opportunity to return to him as his children, a plan that would allow people to choose again—this time to choose to trust him and to let him help them to live life the way he had designed it. But to make that plan work and to eventually bring humanity back to his love and his way, God first had to become judge and disciplinarian.

When things couldn't get any worse, God found one man on the earth who loved him, Noah. God told Noah to build a huge boat, called an *ark*. When it was finished, God sent two of every animal into the ark with Noah's family, and then he sent a flood that covered the whole earth! Forty days and nights later, only those in the ark were still alive.

Noah had children, and grandchildren, and so on, until the earth was populated again. And then God chose one of Noah's descendants, Abraham, and his wife, Sarah, for the next stage of his plan. He told them that he'd be their God and bless them if they trusted and obeyed him. Then he sent Abraham and Sarah on a long trip to a land that he promised to give to their children forever, Canaan, and he promised that one of their descendants would bless the whole world—which was hard to believe, because Abraham and Sarah, who were quite old, hadn't been able to have children.

But God's plan, which would ultimately give everyone the opportunity to become his children again, could become a reality only if God could find people who were willing to trust him and obey him and be the example for others that Adam and Eve had *not* been. Abraham trusted God, and God did the impossible: when Abraham was one hundred and Sarah was ninety, he gave them a son, Isaac.

Isaac's son, Jacob (who was also called Israel), had twelve sons and one daughter. Jacob's favorite son was Joseph, but Joseph's brothers were jealous of him and kidnapped him and sold him as a slave into Egypt. Despite his troubles, Joseph kept trusting and obeying God. Many years later God rewarded that faithfulness by helping Joseph explain a dream to the pharaoh (king) of Egypt, a dream warning that a huge famine was coming. Joseph helped the pharaoh get ready, and when the famine came there was still food in Egypt! Joseph's family came to Egypt for food, and Joseph invited his dad and the rest of his relatives to come and live there.

After the family had lived in Egypt for four hundred years, there were so many Israelites (descendants of Jacob, or Israel) that a new pharaoh—who didn't remember that Joseph had once saved Egypt—got worried! He made the Israelites slaves and ordered all their baby boys killed. Pharaoh's daughter rescued an Israelite baby, Moses, who then grew up in the palace. But when he was forty years old, he killed an Egyptian for beating an Israelite. Moses had to run for his life into the desert, because the pharaoh wanted to kill him.

Years later Moses saw a bush in the desert that burned and burned but didn't burn up. God spoke to him from it: "Go to Egypt and tell Pharaoh to let my people go!" God had saved his chosen family from famine many years earlier by bringing them to Egypt, but now he wanted to return them to Canaan, the land he had given them through Abraham. Moses obeyed, but the pharaoh refused to release the Israelites. God then sent ten plagues on Egypt to help the pharaoh change his mind.

In the last plague, the eldest child in every family was to die. But God told the Israelites to kill lambs, eat them, and put some of the blood on their door frames so that death would pass over their houses. That event was called the Passover.

That very night the pharaoh let the Israelites go. Their departure is known as the Exodus. God led them into the desert and there, on Mount Sinai, he gave Moses the Ten Commandments and the rest of the Law, which told the people how to please God and have a good life. This was second-best to having God as their Father, but knowing some of his principles helped them know how life was supposed to work.

Then God led the Israelites to Canaan. It took forty years before they finally entered the land God had promised to Abraham hundreds of years earlier. Under their new leader, Joshua, the Israelites defeated the wicked people who lived there, and settled in.

When the Israelites followed God's law and trusted him, things went well. When they didn't, their enemies conquered them. Then the Israelites would ask God for help, and God would send a judge (leader) to defeat their enemies and remind the Israelites that they needed to trust and obey God. (One judge God sent was Samson. God gave him amazing strength: he single-handedly defeated a thousand men who came to capture him!)

Then the Israelites asked Samuel, who was a prophet and also the last judge, to ask God to give them a king. Their first king, Saul, fought their enemies, the Philistines. A giant Philistine soldier, Goliath, mocked God and the Israelite army. A young shepherd named David decided to fight him with a sling, stones, and God's help. He won! This young man, who loved and trusted God with all his heart, became the most famous Israelite king. David wrote many of the psalms, and Israel followed his lead in following God.

His son Solomon, who was wise, became a great king as well. He wrote the biblical books known as Proverbs and the Song of Songs. When he got older, Solomon stopped trusting and obeying God, and things started to fall apart again. After Solomon's death his kingdom was divided into two kingdoms: the kingdom of Israel in the north and the kingdom of Judah in the south.

Most of the kings who followed didn't love God as David had and led the people of Israel and Judah away from God. God sent prophets—Isaiah and Jeremiah among them—to remind his people to trust him and follow his law, and to warn them that their enemies would overrun them if they didn't. But the people didn't listen, so the Assyrians wiped out the kingdom of Israel. Then, almost two centuries and many warnings later, the kingdom of Judah was conquered; the people were made prisoners and taken away into exile in faraway Babylon.

One of the people from Judah taken into exile was Daniel, who loved God and became prominent in Babylon. He prayed to God even when it was against Babylon's law. As punishment he was thrown into a large pit full of lions. But God kept Daniel safe because he lived according to God's principles and trusted him!

Some seventy years later the people from Judah were allowed to return to the land God had given them. A priest named Ezra taught them God's Law, and Nehemiah led the Israelites in rebuilding the city walls and gates. Now God's people decided to obey God's Law—for the time being.

That's where the story ends in the first part of the Bible, the Old Testament. The story picks up again four hundred years later in the New Testament:

Everything was ready for the key part of God's plan! God sent an angel to the virgin Mary and her fiancé, Joseph (both descendants of Abraham and Sarah, and of David), who said that Mary would have God's baby and that the whole world would be blessed by him.

Mary had a boy, Jesus, just as God had promised. Jesus was God, but he became a person like us because he loved us and wanted to make a way for us all to return to being God's children. He was God's plan. God told not only Jewish shepherds but also non-Jewish wise men about his Son's birth, showing that Jesus had come for everyone. God worked through the Israelites, but his plan was always for the whole world.

Jesus grew up in Nazareth. When he was about thirty, he began the job God had given him to do: to tell the world about God's love and his plan for them, and to die for them. After Jesus was baptized, God led him into the desert. Satan (remember him?) tempted Jesus to do things his way instead of God's way, just as he had tempted Adam and Eve. But Jesus knew that God's way was best. He refused the temptation and quoted God's words from the Bible as the reason for his refusal.

Jesus chose twelve men to be his special disciples (followers). He taught people about God and his kingdom. He showed people that God loved them by healing the sick and feeding the hungry. He didn't talk about God the punisher of sins; he talked about God's love for humanity and taught people how to be God's children again and trust him.

Jesus also taught that in order to become God's children people need to believe in him, God's only Son. The religious leaders were afraid that the crowds would follow Jesus instead of them. They decided to protect themselves by getting rid of Jesus, but they were afraid of a riot because the people liked him.

Judas, one of Jesus' disciples, offered to help the leaders arrest Jesus quietly, and around the time of the Passover celebration (remember the Passover?) they arrested Jesus at night. Jesus was put on trial for blasphemy, because he said that he was God's Son. The punishment was death. Jesus was beaten and then led out to be crucified—a horrible death. Jesus asked his Father to forgive the people because they didn't know what they were doing. Then he said, "It's finished." He'd done everything God sent him to do!

But Jesus was God's Son. Though Jesus had been born human, God was his Father, so he wasn't separated from God like all other humans. Jesus was like the innocent Passover lambs that had died so that others could live. He died in the place of Adam and Eve and of every person who has been born since, so that we can know God again as our Father.

After Jesus died, friends put his body in a nearby tomb. The Jewish leaders asked that the tomb be guarded so that no one could steal Jesus' body and say he'd risen from the dead as he'd said he would. But on the third day the tomb was empty! Jesus then appeared to over five hundred people, proving that he was alive again. God had accepted his death (instead of ours) as payment for our sins, but because Jesus had no sin of his own, death couldn't hold him. The separation begun by Adam and Eve had come to an end. All people could be God's children again!

The last instruction Jesus gave his disciples was to go and tell all people around the world that they could again make the choice to become God's children. Jesus sent the Holy Spirit to help his disciples and followers tell the world about him. The religious leaders tried to stop them, but their efforts failed. Thousands and thousands of people heard the news and began to love, trust, and obey God.

One of the religious leaders, Saul, searched for Jesus' followers so that he could have them killed. But one day Jesus appeared to Saul (who thought Jesus was still dead) and asked him why he was persecuting the Son of God. From that day forward, Saul became one of Jesus' most famous followers. Saul, better known as Paul, traveled around the world telling people about Jesus. He started churches and wrote letters to help God's new children, called Christians, in their efforts to get to know God and live as God wanted them to. He also explained the teachings of the Bible and showed why Jesus' life and death were so important. His letters make up part of the New Testament.

Many years after Jesus went back to heaven and the Christian church had grown and spread all over the world, the Apostle John was sent to prison for his faith and Jesus gave him a message for the church. It's found in the last book of the Bible, Revelation. In that book Jesus promises to come back and take us to be with him. There will be a new heaven and a new earth, where there will be no more sadness or tears or pain, but only love and happiness. We'll be with God as his children, just as he planned before the world began. And we'll get to see and live the awesome things that God had in mind when he first made Adam and Eve!

That's the Big Story. Once your children understand that overall story, they'll have a context for everything else they read and learn, and the things you teach them will begin to mutually enhance and reinforce each other.

Bible storybooks often have two flaws. First, in their zeal to include the majority of the Bible's well-known narratives, they often end up with stories that are too short. Our children prefer longer stories so that they have a chance to get involved in the characters and the plot (and so that they can keep us reading longer!). Many Bible storybooks also fail to link the individual stories together or put them into the context of the Big Story of the Bible. But when we read to our children from a Bible storybook, we can compensate for these flaws by linking the short stories together and talking about where they fit into the Big Story. For example, most Bible storybooks contain several stories in which Moses is the central character. Reading these together as a unit will help hold your children's interest, because some of the characters appear again and again; and the unit as a whole can then be placed in the context of the Bible's overall storyline. With this strategy, your children's interest in and understanding of the material will be increased.

If you'd like to go through a Bible storybook with your children and explain the overall story, here is a suggested list of stories that should be read in sequence. Leave the other stories for the next time through. All the stories about the following characters and events can be read as part of an overview:

- Creation
- Adam and Eve
- Cain and Abel
- Noah and the flood
- Abraham
- Isaac, Jacob, Joseph
- Moses
- Joshua
- Deborah, Gideon, Samson (judges)
- Samuel
- Saul
- David
- Solomon
- Jonah
- Taken to Babylon (Babylonian Exile)
- Daniel
- The return from Babylon
- Nehemiah
- Jesus and all New Testament stories

When your children move from Bible storybooks into a whole-text Bible, the foundation you've laid with such an overview will give them a context and a structure on which to build everything else they learn.[1]

---

[1]*The Amazing Treasure Bible Storybook,* published by Zondervan and available through your local bookstore, is designed to give your children an overview. This book is especially good for children between the ages of six and twelve. For more information on this and other materials that can help you, visit our Web site at *http://www.lightwavepublishing.com.*

What can I do to help my kids get a handle on how all the pieces of the Bible fit together?

When your children want to move from their Bible storybook to a "regular" Bible, it's time to begin talking to them about how the Bible was put together. At first glance the structure looks confusing, but there's a definite, easy-to-grasp plan and order in the arrangement of the books of the Bible. If you're not already familiar with this information, review it so that you can begin to progressively teach it to your children.

The Bible Is a Library

The Bible isn't just one big book; it's a library of sixty-six books. And like a library, it's organized in sections, each section with its own kind of books.

The Bible's library is broken down into two main sections, the Old Testament and the New Testament, each with its own subsections. (Some Bibles contain a third section, called the Apocrypha. We'll talk briefly about those books later, but for now we'll concentrate on the sixty-six books in the two sections that are common to all Bibles.)

The Old Testament contains the books that tell the story of creation and give the history of God's chosen people, the Israelites. It also contains nonhistory books, such as poetic books and books by prophets, that were written during this same time period.

The New Testament contains the books that tell the story of Jesus—his birth, life, death, resurrection, and return to heaven—as well as the story of what the disciples did afterward and the beginnings of the church. The New Testament also contains books that were written by the apostles and other early church leaders; these books teach us what it means to be, and how to live as, Christians.

THE OLD TESTAMENT

The easiest way to help kids understand and remember how the Old Testament is organized is to use the

5 – 12 – 5 – 5 – 12

breakdown. These numbers represent the number of Bible books in each section of the Old Testament and are easy to remember:

5	books of the Law
12	books of history
5	books of poetry
5	Major Prophets
12	Minor Prophets

Here's what you'll find in each section:

5 Books of the Law

Genesis, Exodus, Leviticus, Numbers, and Deuteronomy

These books are called "the Law" because they contain the Ten Commandments and all the other details of the Jewish Law that God gave to Moses and the Israelites. But they also tell a major portion of the Big Story:

- Creation
- Adam and Eve
- Cain and Abel
- Noah
- Abraham
- Isaac
- Jacob (Israel)
- Joseph
- Moses
- Exodus
- The Israelites' wilderness wandering

12 Books of History

Joshua, Judges, Ruth, 1 and 2 Samuel, 1 and 2 Kings, 1 and 2 Chronicles, Ezra, Nehemiah, and Esther

These books cover the Big Story from when Joshua took over leadership of the Israelites after Moses died, until the return of the Israelites from captivity in Babylon. The main stories covered in this section include:

- Joshua
- Deborah, Gideon, Samson (judges)
- Ruth
- Samuel
- Saul
- David
- Solomon
- The divided kingdom
- Elijah
- Assyria's devastation of Israel
- Judah's captivity and exile in Babylon
- The return to Jerusalem
- The reinstitution of the Law by Ezra
- The rebuilding of the wall by Nehemiah
- Esther

The history covered in this section takes us to the end of the Old Testament time period. The remaining twenty-two books of the Old Testament were all written during the time covered in these twelve books of history, but they're not history books and they're not in chronological order.

So once you've finished the book of Esther and you go to the next book, Job, you're no longer reading chronologically. More important, you're reading a very different kind of book than the ones you've read thus far in the Old Testament.

5 Books of Poetry

Job, Psalms, Proverbs, Ecclesiastes, and the Song of Songs

The books that make up this section of the library consist of poetry and wisdom writings (books of proverbs and wise sayings). These books were written during the time period covered in the twelve history books, as I noted earlier. All five books are a departure from the main storyline, but they give us insight into some of the characters who were involved in Big Story events. In addition, these books contain wonderful instructions about life and insights into our relationship with God.

Three of the poetic books—Job, Ecclesiastes, and the Song of Songs—deal with very adult concepts. Job tackles the issue of why a good, loving God sometimes allows bad things to happen to good people. Ecclesiastes deals with the problem that life as we know it can seem meaningless. The Song of Songs deals with romantic love and the resulting emotional and physical relationship between a man and a woman.

The two remaining books—Psalms and Proverbs—are awesome books for our children to read. The book of Psalms was largely written by David and deals very honestly with our personal relationship with God. The book of Proverbs was written largely by Solomon and is addressed to young people who are learning how life works. It's full of practical wisdom about God's principles and offers guidance in how to put them into practice in every area of life, from friendship to finance, from attitude to work ethic.

5 Major Prophets

Isaiah, Jeremiah, Lamentations, Ezekiel, and Daniel

12 Minor Prophets

Hosea, Joel, Amos, Obadiah, Jonah, Micah, Nahum, Habakkuk, Zephaniah, Haggai, Zechariah, and Malachi

The last two sections of the Old Testament, the Major Prophets and Minor Prophets, all record the words and actions of prophets whom God sent to speak to Israel and Judah during the time of the kings and thereafter, until shortly after the return of the Jews from Babylon. A prophet was a person who sought the mind of God and delivered God's specific words or message to the Israelites and their rulers. These words were usually warnings of the bad things that would happen if the Israelites continued to ignore God's Law, but there was also the promise that God would bless them once again.

BETWEEN THE TESTAMENTS

There's a four-hundred-year gap between the end of the history covered by the Old Testament and the beginning of the New Testament. Many Bibles today give a brief summary of this time period between the books of Malachi and Matthew. A lot of things changed during those four hundred years, and it's helpful for kids to know, for example, how the Romans got to be in charge, where the Pharisees and Sadducees came from, and why synagogues were invented—developments that hadn't happened yet at the end of the Old Testament.

Some Bibles contain a set of books between Malachi and Matthew called the Apocrypha. Everything in the Apocrypha, with the exception of 2 Esdras, was written during this four-hundred-year period between the Old and New Testaments. Ever since the days of the early church, there's been some difference of opinion as to whether these books belong in the Bible or not. Although they're included in many Bibles, there's general agreement—even among churches that include them in their Bibles—that the apocryphal books don't have the same level of authority as the sixty-six books everyone agrees on. When teaching children, it's therefore probably best to focus on the sixty-six books that are common to all Bibles.

Young people can read and study the Apocrypha on their own if they choose to when they're older. (Two of the apocryphal books, 1 and 2 Maccabees, tell part of the story of what happened during the four hundred years between the Testaments. These make for interesting, if at times rather violent, reading.) If you decide you want to introduce your children to the Apocrypha, read through the various books first so that you can steer young readers through or past some of the more graphic content.

THE NEW TESTAMENT

The section of the library that makes up the New Testament is relatively straightforward. Here's a simple

> **4 – 1 – 14 – 7 – 1**

breakdown of the New Testament books that's easy for kids to remember, especially if it's said with a little rhythm:

4	gospels
1	book of history
14	letters by the Apostle Paul
7	"general letters" by others
1	book of prophecy

4 Gospels

Matthew, Mark, Luke, and John

These books are four separate accounts of the life of Jesus. Matthew and John were two of Jesus' disciples, so their gospels are eyewitness accounts. The book of Mark was written by John Mark, who was a close associate of the Apostle Peter and wrote down Peter's stories about his years with Jesus. The gospel of Luke was written by the Apostle Paul's trusted companion and physician, Luke, who based his gospel on the testimony of eyewitnesses and the preaching and stories of the apostles about their years with Jesus. (Jesus' twelve disciples were called *apostles* after Jesus went back to heaven.) Luke also wrote the book of Acts.

1 Book of History

Acts

The book of Acts (short for Acts of the Apostles) is a history of the first thirty years of the Christian church. It was written by Luke, who also wrote one of the gospels. The gospel of Luke and the book of Acts together are one seamless history of the life of Jesus and the initial growth of the church that followed. The book of Acts begins in Jerusalem, with Jesus' last words to his disciples, and ends with the Apostle Paul in Rome, where his life and ministry would end. Most of the other books in the New Testament were written during the thirty-year period covered in Acts.

14 Letters of Paul

Romans, 1 and 2 Corinthians, Galatians, Ephesians, Philippians, Colossians, 1 and 2 Thessalonians, 1 and 2 Timothy, Titus, Philemon, and Hebrews

7 General Letters

James, 1 and 2 Peter, 1 and 2 and 3 John, and Jude

These two sections contain letters that the Apostle Paul and other apostles and church leaders wrote to some of the first Christian churches and/or to the leaders of those churches. These letters (also known as *epistles*) were written to instruct and guide Christians and churches and are, of course, still very relevant for us today. They are, in fact, the primary place where we should look for help with getting to know God and living the life God desires for us.

The books in these sections are arranged not chronologically but by length, from the longest to the shortest. The only exception is Hebrews, which is the last of the books in the section of Paul's letters. Although it's widely believed that Hebrews was written by Paul, no one is absolutely sure. Therefore, this book was placed at the end of Paul's letters and just before the general letters (so named because most of them weren't addressed to particular churches or people).

1 Book of Prophecy

Revelation

Most Bible scholars believe this book was written by the Apostle John, one of Jesus' disciples, who also wrote one of the gospels and three of the New Testament letters (1, 2, and 3 John). Revelation is an apocalyptic book: it contains a great deal of symbolism and represents future events. It can be a difficult read, because the meanings and interpretations of the fantastic pictures and visions described aren't given in the book.

Much has been written about what these visions mean. Many people believe that the majority of the events outlined will take place just before Jesus' return to earth. But it's easy to get so wrapped up in the details that we miss the focus of the book. We're encouraged by John to stay strong in our faith, even in the face of persecution, and to continue in our efforts to know and trust God and his love because this present age will come to an end. Jesus is coming back, God will judge mankind, and his children will live with him forever in a new heaven and earth.

By way of summary, here's an easy way to remember how the Old Testament and the New Testament are structured:

OLD TESTAMENT 5 – 12 – 5 – 5 – 12	NEW TESTAMENT 4 – 1 – 14 – 7 – 1
HISTORICAL BOOKS	
5 BOOKS OF LAW 12 BOOKS OF HISTORY	4 GOSPELS 1 BOOK OF HISTORY
MISCELLANEOUS BOOKS	
5 POETIC/WISDOM BOOKS	14 LETTERS OF PAUL 7 GENERAL LETTERS
PROPHETIC BOOKS	
5 MAJOR PROPHETS 12 MINOR PROPHETS	1 BOOK OF PROPHECY

What are some practical tips for reading the Bible to or with my kids?

The first part of this chapter provided the background your children need to read and understand the Bible. Here are some hints and tips that will help you read the Bible with your children or help you show them how to read it on their own:

Reading with an Attitude

Your own attitude toward the Bible is contagious; it will likely become your children's attitude. Respect God's Word as a practical guide to life rather than treating it as an obscure religious handbook that sits quietly on a shelf gathering dust. When you're making decisions as a family, helping your children make their own decisions, or feeling curious about how something in life works—saving money, for example—look up what the Bible says. When you're teaching your children life principles such as honesty and kindness, anchor what you're teaching with actual verses from the Bible.

But be careful not to refer to the Bible only when things are serious. Allow it to become a normal and everyday part of your life—a constant, practical, helpful reference that's used daily. The Bible should be as natural a guide for life as *TV Guide* is for television. If you're just beginning this process, start slowly and build. You'll have your whole family running for cover if you go from little or no Bible study straight to biblical blitz with both barrels blazing. The best first step is to sit down and talk to your children about what the Bible is, what it teaches, and what role it should play in people's lives. Talk to them about beginning to use it as the instruction manual for life in your family, and move forward with everyone working together. It's this daily access that keeps God's wisdom working in our children's hearts and minds.

Fish That Eat People and Donkeys That Talk

God gave us a book full of marvelous stories about kings and peasants, battles and miracles, fish that swallow people, donkeys that talk, and so on. He didn't give us a dry-as-dust book of rules and guidelines. In the Bible, God gave us a wonderful variety of literary forms, including poetry, visions, and proverbs—but especially stories that bring life's guidebook to life and make it more interesting and effective.

> The Bible stories are meant to teach us and our children, but if we're continually light on the story and heavy on the lesson, we'll end up light on the effect.

Kids will forget some of our applications and lessons, no matter how sincere our efforts and their intentions, long before they forget the stories. These stories are meant to teach us and our children, but if we're continually light on the story and heavy on the lesson, we'll end up light on the effect. Be content to simply read the stories to your younger children, letting the lessons come in response to questions and to situations that give you an appropriate parallel.

It's important to involve both sides of the brain in the biblical process—the left brain for explanations, the right brain for images and stories. Especially for some kids, stories are the best teaching tool by far. If we as parents learn to *enjoy* the stories of the Bible *as stories* before we draw all kinds of applications, we'll help our kids build a reservoir on which they can draw in daily life—and on which we can draw when we talk with them about God's instruction manual.

A Bill of Rights (and Wrongs)

We should make a point of teaching our kids that the Bible contains the truth about how life works. One of the greatest parenting benefits the Bible provides is a solid foundation for teaching children what's right. When we teach our children that there's a right and a wrong way of doing things, we imply that there are unchanging principles and absolute truths that govern life. If, on the other hand, we teach them without substantiating our claim that what we're teaching is truth, that it comes from God, we set the stage for someone else to come along and convince them of the opposite. If God didn't create things to function a certain way, then everything is random and a matter of opinion, and telling our children that they have to be honest becomes merely our opinion of what they should do.

If there's no absolute right or wrong, then our children could decide that lying consistently makes more sense to them than truth-telling and is the way that they want to live their lives. If truth is subjective and random, who are we to tell our children how they should behave? It's our opinion against theirs. We may tell them, "This is how it's going to be as long as you're under my roof," but that doesn't prepare them for life; it just prolongs the inevitable.

Lessons from the Everyday

Since the Bible's teachings are instructions for life, everyday life is the ideal classroom. When we're teaching our children the principles that govern life, whether about attitude, behavior, integrity, work ethic, sibling relationships, or anything else, we should refer them to what the Bible teaches, emphasizing that the Bible is life's manual.

The Boredom Bugaboo

Kids love adventure and variety. Be careful not to fall into a rut, following the same pattern over and over again in your Bible time. With young kids, consider buying or renting some animated Bible story videos and using them as a special once-a-week replacement for the regular Bible story or reading. Use a Bible storybook on CD-ROM for a few nights or consider using a different Bible storybook or Bible. Or sit in a different spot—in the kitchen, for example, having some milk and cookies—while you're reading the story.

With older children who are reading on their own, variety may be even more important. Offer to read to them every once in a while. Rent a movie such as *The Ten Commandments* or suggest alternative Christian literature for a change. Try calling the whole family together to read a Bible story or portion of the Bible. If at any time your children start to get bored or begin to lose interest in the process, examine your presentation and change what you're doing or mix in some variety to bring the excitement level up again.

When You Don't Feel Like the Energizer Bunny . . .

Variety can be the spice of Bible learning for kids, but a parent with a little energy and excitement can also go a long way. If Bible time with our kids is scheduled at the end of the day and we're tired, it's easy to rush through or even skip it—or, worse yet, get cranky about it or bored with it ourselves. Before going to read with your children, remember how important this activity is and try your best to gather up enough energy to make it a memorable experience. If you're just too exhausted, some creativity and/or variety will help. Bring out the animated Bible video or suggest that an older brother or sister read with the younger ones. Alternatively, if your spouse is involved in the teaching process, ask him or her to take over for the evening. The best way to help your children in the process is to be upbeat and spontaneous. Don't rush; stop frequently for questions; hide the book periodically and ask your kids simple trivia questions about what you just read; praise them for their correct answers; and make the occasion special by spending a little extra time with them once the nightly prayer and Bible time is finished.

Habits Aren't Only for Nuns

It's important that we not only teach our children from the Bible but also help them establish a regular habit of Bible reading. Let your children know that Bible reading is something all of us should do most every day of our lives. It's not just entertainment; it's one of the foundations for a successful life. Help your children of all ages develop and continue in this daily habit. Let your older children choose when they'd like to read their Bibles during the day, and then

> **One of the best ways to reinforce the value and importance of regularity in Bible reading and study is to demonstrate this daily habit yourself.**

encourage them to stick with that schedule. And help your children dedicate a little more time to their Bible reading as they grow older.

One of the best ways to reinforce the value and importance of regularity in Bible reading and study is to demonstrate this daily habit yourself. Purposely choose a time for your own Bible reading and study when your children will know where you are and what you're doing. A great way to encourage your older children in their Bible exploration is to talk to them occasionally about what you're reading and learning and how what you're learning is affecting your life.

Some Simple Suggestions

Encourage your children to pray an informal prayer before they start reading, asking God to teach them and help them understand and apply what they read. Also—and this goes against everything in our high-speed culture—encourage them to slow down and think about what they're reading, and even to talk with God about things that strike them or that they don't understand.

Teach them that reading our Bibles should be like a treasure hunt. We're looking for the golden nuggets of truth that are the keys to making our lives all that our loving Father created them to be. Racing through the Bible is merely reading a great book; learning from it and from God takes a little time and concentration.

You can help your children learn the skill of slowing down and reflecting on what the stories mean while they're young, when you're reading to them from a Bible storybook. Allow your young children to interrupt with questions, and take the time to answer them. When you see an important application in the story, briefly mention it before going on. In addition, discuss the story when you're finished; don't just close the book and rush on to something else. This will help your children focus on the purpose of the activity, which is to allow our Father in heaven to teach us his principles for life and help us to be all that we can be. (Remember not to force a lesson. Sometimes talking about what you've read means just talking about the *story*.)

Tool Time!

Most of us aren't familiar enough with the Bible to be able to remember key verses for all of life's topics (or, if we remember them, to be able to find them). Therefore, the best way to teach your older children how to get at the wisdom of Scripture is to begin searching out these topics for yourself *with* them. If you want to teach your children what the Bible says about telling the truth, for example, you can sit down with them—with your Bible and theirs, along with one or more Bible reference tools—and look up and discuss together what the Bible says. Going through that process is a great way to reinforce that the Bible is life's instruction manual.

Let's say your kids want to find out what the Bible says about forgiveness. In a regular book you'd look in the index at the back under *forgiveness* or *forgive,* and you'd find the places in the book that deal with forgiveness. You follow similar steps with the Bible. Listed below are some of the features you'll find in many Bibles, with suggestions on how you can benefit from them.

- If you want to find all the places where a particular word is found in the Bible, you can use a *concordance,* which is an index of most words used in the Bible. A full-fledged concordance is a book in its own right, but some Bibles have a simplified concordance in the back to help you find verses that contain key words (such as *forgiveness*).
- But a concordance won't tell you where to find verses that talk about forgiveness but don't use the actual word (such as, for example, the story of the Prodigal Son in Luke 15:11–24). To find these verses you need a *topical index,* which lists the verses that deal with a particular topic. Although the topical index may be a separate section in your Bible, it's more likely that index entries for various topics will be scattered in different places throughout the Bible. (In that case, there may be a list of the topics and where you can find them in the front of the Bible.)

The cross-references found in the margins or in a center column in some Bibles are often simplified topical index entries. If you follow the cross-references from one verse to the next, to the next, and so on, you can sometimes study a whole topic.

There are also tools that explain the *meaning* of things in the Bible:

- A *Bible dictionary* explains the meaning of specific words and concepts in the Bible. For example, in the back of the New International Reader's Version (NIrV) is a very brief dictionary that includes the entry "Grace: God's kindness to human beings. It is given without being earned." Bible dictionaries are also helpful in giving you more information and background on people and places.
- A *Bible commentary* explains what particular verses or sections mean.

In many Bibles, especially study Bibles, you'll find notes that give you a bit of both—explanations of words and of the meaning of verses or sections. These notes often lead you to other related verses and help you explain the verses more clearly to your children.

Finally, there are tools that help you understand the *background and structure* of the Bible.

- Many Bibles have an *introduction* to each Bible book that gives the background of the book, explains where the book fits in the Bible as a whole, and gives an overview of what the book is about.
- Many Bibles also have *maps* that help clarify the geographical setting of each Bible story. (Incidentally, it can be fascinating—and can help your children understand how real the Bible stories are—to locate biblical countries and places on a modern map. Babylonia seems far away in time and space; Iraq does not.)

If you choose children's and youth Bibles that contain some of these features in simplified form, your children can begin to dig for truth.

To go even further in helping your children find out what the Bible says about life's many topics, buy a good study Bible for yourself that contains many of these features in abridged form. The *NIV Study Bible*, for example, has a concordance, a Bible dictionary, maps, a commentary in the form of explanatory notes at the bottom of the page, cross-references, and Bible book introductions.

As you go further in your own studies, and to help explain things to your children, you may want to buy more complete reference works in separate books. (Keep in mind that a concordance is really an index to all the words in a specific *translation* of the Bible. For example, *Strong's Concordance* is an index to the King James Version, while the *NIV Concordance* is an index to the New International Version.)

The life and teachings of Jesus in the gospels contain the most straightforward presentation of who God is and how we should live our lives.

How can I help my kids read through the Bible?

Here are some suggestions to help your children read through the Bible.

First-time Reading: A Gospel

When your children are old enough to want to read the Bible for themselves but too young to find their way through it, have them read one or more of the gospels. These books should be regular reading for children. The life and teachings of Jesus in the gospels contain the most straightforward presentation of who God is and how we should live our lives.

Luke might be the best gospel to start with, since it includes the story of Jesus' birth and also a lot of parables and miracles. John's gospel is a bit more challenging: your children may need some help, especially with the long discourse in chapters 14 through 17. Encourage your older children, after they've read some or all of the gospels a few times, to read them again, now focusing not just on the story but on what Jesus taught and how that teaching applies to their own life.

If you have younger kids and are still reading Bible stories with them or to them, read the stories that cover the life of Jesus more often than the rest of the stories.

Through the Bible: First Round

When your children are ready to read through the Bible on their own, it's helpful to give them some guidance, especially the first time through. The reading program suggested here for the first round focuses mainly on the history contained in the Bible, especially in the Old Testament.

A word of caution if you've never read the Bible: there are some parts of the Old Testament that record wars and other not-so-nice real-life historical events. If your children are still quite young when they want to read the Bible for themselves, you may want to read along with them (or ahead of them) so that you can recommend skipping questionable parts or be ready to explain them.

On a related topic, the issue of violence in the Old Testament may bring up the question of the contradiction that seems to exist between the way God is pictured in the New Testament and the way he's pictured in the Old Testament.

Here are three things that you can explain to your children to help them with this question:

- God is love, but he's also our judge. Our love for our children compels us to discipline them and punish wrong behavior so that they'll learn right from wrong now and not have to suffer greater consequences later in life. Similarly, God, in his love, must punish those who choose to do things wrong, for their sake and for the sake of everyone else.
- The Bible is a progressive revelation of who God is. In other words, those who recorded the events of the Old Testament recorded them accurately but with a growing and progressive understanding of God, his character, and his motivation. God was seen and pictured in the Old Testament more as the punisher of evil than as our loving Father. We know now that who God is, is most accurately demonstrated by Jesus' life, and that's where we should focus when trying to understand who he is.
- The people of the Old Testament didn't have the same kind of relationship with God that we have. Jesus said, "What I'm about to tell you is true. No one more important than John the Baptist has ever been born. But the least important person in the kingdom of heaven is more important than he is" (Matthew 11:11). In other words, Jesus' death and resurrection allowed us to be restored to our originally intended relationship with God and become his children. It's incorrect to try to understand or apply the way that God is depicted in the Old Testament to our lives as Christians today or to our relationship with him.

OLD TESTAMENT

Your children will want to touch on each of the major subsections of the Old Testament as they proceed through the Bible on their own for the first time. Here are some suggestions for how they might approach the various subsections.

5 Books of Law

Most children will want to read the history portions only. The sections that are mostly laws aren't particularly interesting for kids. Read Genesis; Exodus 1–20, 23–24, 32–40; Numbers 8–36; and Deuteronomy 1–11 and 34.

12 Books of History

Out of these twelve books, the only ones you might want to encourage your children to skip are 1 and 2 Chronicles. Although these two books contain some new material, they're basically a repeat of the historical period already covered by Samuel and Kings. (They're worthwhile reading the second time through, however.) The books of Ruth and Esther will seem a little out of place in the flow of the story. Fortunately, most Bibles today provide an introduction to each Bible book. Help your children get into the habit of reading the introduction first; then they'll know how books such as Ruth and Esther fit in.

5 Books of Poetry

If you read through these books yourself and want to help your older children read and understand them, the exercise could be very beneficial. However, these books don't follow the historical sequence, as I noted earlier; and Job, Ecclesiastes, and the Song of Songs deal with subject matter kids may not understand on their own. You may want to suggest that they skip these books the first time (or even the first few times) through their Bible.

If your children are reading through the history portions of their Bible, encourage them to read one chapter from Psalms and one chapter from Proverbs along with each session's history reading. Reading straight through these books all at once can be too much of a good thing. If even the reduced load is too much reading, have them alternate one chapter from Psalms and one chapter from Proverbs—one each session. They'll go through Proverbs close to five times for each time they go through Psalms, but that's okay: Proverbs is a more practical, life-related book.

5 Major Prophets and 12 Minor Prophets

Although much of what's contained in these books wouldn't be very beneficial or easy to understand for children, you can direct your kids to a few passages as they do their history reading. For instance, the book of Jonah is a classic Bible story that makes great reading for youngsters. (It's especially interesting to note where Jonah fits in the context of the Big Story. God had been warning the Israelites for some time that their enemies would defeat them if they didn't follow God's principles and trust him for help. Assyria had already begun the process of moving in on the Israelites. Nineveh, the city where God sent Jonah to preach, was the capital city of Assyria. Knowing that makes it easier to understand why Jonah ran the other way.)

The first seven chapters of the book of Daniel also make good reading. (Daniel was a Jewish captive in the kingdom of Babylon and was elevated to different positions of leadership under at least three kings because he put God and his principles first in his life.) It would also be beneficial to have your children read Isaiah 52 and 53 so that they can see how the prophets told about Jesus hundreds of years before his birth. (In Luke 22:37 Jesus quotes from this portion of Scripture and says that it talks about him.)

The other books in this section are better read once the overall story has been finished so that the context of these books can be understood. (If you've never read these books yourself, give them a try. They're fascinating, and they fill in more details of the story that's covered in the history section. Be sure to read the Bible book introductions too so that you understand where the books fit in the context of the Big Story.)

NEW TESTAMENT

4 Gospels

The gospels should be counted as the number-one priority for Bible reading material for children. When kids are reading through the entire history of the Bible, however, it's best that they pick just one gospel to read in that process, since all four gospels cover the same time period.

1 Book of History

Acts gives the historical framework for all of the books of the New Testament beyond the four gospels, and whenever your children read through one of the gospels, they should follow it up with the book of Acts. When they've read all four gospels and Acts, they've completed the historical portion of the New Testament.

14 Letters of Paul

7 General Letters

Since these books are so important to our lives and faith, it's beneficial to add at least parts of some of these books to the basic history reading. On your child's first time through, add, for example, Romans 8:18–39; 1 Corinthians 13; Ephesians 1:3–14; Philippians 1:15–23; James 2; and/or other selections you may want them to read.

1 Book of Prophecy

The last two chapters of Revelation, 21 and 22, talk a little about what it will be like for us after the end of this age and the second coming of Jesus. These chapters make a great ending for your children's reading of the Bible story.

When your children enter their teens, they'll probably be drawn to this book and read the rest of it on their own. Because of its mysteries, its visions, and the fact that it somehow reveals history that hasn't yet happened, it's very intriguing.

Through the Bible: Second Round

As your children start through the Bible for the second time, suggest that they add 1 and 2 Chronicles in the Old Testament. In the New Testament, suggest that they read a different gospel and add either more selections from the letters or, if you think they're ready to read whole epistles, add Romans, Galatians, James, and 1 John. Again, remember to have your children read the book introductions to help them find the historical context.

Through the Bible: Third Round

Kids can, of course, repeat round one or round two. Alternatively, they can read through the entire Bible in less than a year (approximately two hundred readings) if each reading consists of

* Two chapters from the Old Testament (selected from Genesis; Exodus 1–20, 23–24, 32–40; Numbers 8–36; Deuteronomy 1–11 and 34; Joshua; Judges; Ruth; 1 and 2 Samuel; 1 and 2 Kings; 1 and 2 Chronicles; Isaiah 52 and 53; Jonah; Daniel 1–7; Ezra; Nehemiah; and Esther)
* One chapter from the New Testament (selected from one gospel and all of the rest of the New Testament)

- One Psalm
- One chapter from Proverbs

Using this strategy, your children should finish the Old and New Testaments and Psalms at roughly the same time, while rotating through Proverbs approximately five times.

Is there value in having my kids memorize verses from the Bible?

Anyone who ever attended a Bible class or Sunday school class as a child remembers memorizing Bible verses and receiving candy or some other sort of prize for doing so. Our kids are doing the same, and we as parents are proud of our children when we hear them recite their verses, and we will often help them memorize them word for word. But what's the point of memorizing Bible verses?

Here's a picture that will help our children understand

why and how it's beneficial for them to memorize Scripture. Say your son gets hired by an NBA team to play basketball. After the contract is signed, the coach hands him a thick book—the strategy and play manual—and tells him to go over it thoroughly so that he can play in next week's game.

The first thing he'll do is read it through from cover to cover to get an idea of the team's overall approach and strategy. But then he'll need to go back over certain parts and study them. He'll read and reread those parts and think about them so that he'll know and understand what to do on the court. But he'll also memorize the different plays so that he'll know exactly what to do in each situation. In brief, he'll read for general understanding, study the important parts, and memorize key plays so that he'll know what to do in specific situations.

That's how we should treat the Bible—as the strategy and play manual for our lives. We should read it for a general understanding of life, study specific parts and topics so that we know how to function in life, and memorize key portions so that when life's circumstances put us on the spot we'll know what to do.

Receiving candy and prizes for memorizing Bible verses can be motivating, but if those rewards are the only reason for learning verses, we might as well have our kids memorize Shakespeare. Psalm 119:11 says that the Bible is a lamp to our feet and a light to our path. The

> **There's no brownie-point system in heaven that rewards our children for the number of Bible verses they can recite perfectly. It's far more important that our children memorize the meaning, intent, and purpose of a Bible verse than it is for them to memorize its exact wording.**

instructions in the Bible give us direction and help us make decisions. We should help our children memorize key verses—and make sure that they understand them—so that when particular situations arise they'll know how to respond.

There's no brownie-point system in heaven that rewards our children for the number of Bible verses they can recite perfectly. It's far more important that our children memorize the meaning, intent, and purpose of a Bible verse than it is for them to memorize its exact wording.

The best verses to memorize with your children are the ones that you looked up together when you were trying to learn and understand one of life's principles. If your children are learning memory verses somewhere else and bringing them home, spend a little time with them to make sure that they understand what each verse means and how they can apply it. You'll find that their ability to memorize the actual words will increase drastically with practice. If you want to find key verses for your children to memorize, use one of the Bible reference tools found in the back of most Bibles, such as a topical study guide or a concordance.

3
·

Church

~~~~~~

A. Can I raise good kids who believe in God without taking them to church?

B. What's the purpose of church, and how can it help my children?

C. Isn't there a right and a wrong way for a church to believe and teach? Is it important to take my children to a certain church?

D. My spouse and I come from different church backgrounds. How can we agree on where to take the children to church?

E. What about special services for children, such as baptism, dedication, and confirmation? Are these an important part of my children's spiritual development?

~~~~~~

Can I raise good kids who believe in God without taking them to church?

DOES OUR CHURCH HAVE A SERVICE BEFORE BREAKFAST? MAX AND I ARE UP ANYWAY.

We want our children to get to know God as their Father and to have him teach them, guide them, direct them, and care and provide for them. One tool that we've already talked about that's essential in this process is the Bible. Church is another tool that facilitates the same goal in very specific and extremely helpful ways.

Many of us had bad or just plain boring experiences in church as kids. Now we wonder if there's any point to taking our children through the same process. Is church really worth sacrificing Sunday mornings in bed for? Isn't there an easier way to give our children whatever benefits church attendance is supposed give them? And if in spite of our own bad memories we *are* attending church with our children, we wonder if it's possible to make the experience better and more meaningful for them then it was for us.

According to a Gallup poll conducted in August 1997 for CNN and *USA Today*,

- 89% of those surveyed said that religion was either very important or fairly important in their lives.
- 68% said that they were members at the church or synagogue where they attended religious services.
- Only 41% said that they attended religious services regularly (with an additional 29% saying that they attended, but seldom).
- And only 35% said that they'd attended a religious service in the last seven days.

These figures highlight a definite discrepancy between the number of people who believe that they should go to church and the number who actually make it out of that comfy bed on a regular basis. Maybe we as a society aren't really sure anymore just why it's good to go to church.

First, let's put church into perspective. Going to church is something—one of the *many* things—we as Christians *do;* it's not something that defines who we *are*. The fact that we believe in God and are Christians doesn't necessarily mean that we go to church. And the fact that we go to church doesn't necessarily mean that we're Christians—just as sitting in a garage wouldn't mean that we're cars.

If the only reason we go to church is for the sake of appearances, or to get brownie points with God, or because it's what we're *supposed* to do—and if that's why we take (or send!) our children to church—I can pretty well guarantee that in the future they'll want to sleep in on Sunday mornings.

We don't send our children to school so that people will think they're smart, or because we feel it's the right thing to do, or to get brownie points with the school superintendent. We send them to school so that they'll learn basic skills and knowledge that will prepare them for the rest of their lives. Knowing why we send our children to school and helping them understand why they have to go is critical; when things get hard or boring in the classroom, that understanding provides the motivation and the goal that keeps them going.

Imagine the world a hundred years from now. Technology has advanced to the point that no one needs to work. Intellectual issues are discussed only by a few old-fashioned people who still hold to the antiquated notion that we need to put and store information in our brains. But our children are still going to school—because it's always been that way.

If that future world were real, at some point somebody would undoubtedly question the relevance of sending kids to school. What would school be accomplishing, after all, except serving as a somewhat useful form of child care? And then voices of reform would argue that an institution without a clear purpose should be abolished.

Where does that argument leave the church? Untouched. Because going to church isn't an end in itself. If it were, we might as well stay in our warm beds with the Sunday paper and a cup of coffee. But the church *does* serve a purpose, and it can and should be a practical and real help in our lives and in our children's lives.

Before going any further, we need to establish a foundational truth: *church is God's idea*. Our church experience as children may have made us wonder sometimes if it was one of God's *better* ideas, but the fact remains: church is God's idea. It's easy to lose sight of this basic truth. With all the different churches that want our attendance, involvement, and support, we've gotten the idea that attending church is like going to professional sports events or movies: we expect to be well entertained. If the entertainers do a great job, we'll go back, and our attendance and support will help make the church successful. But that's the wrong approach. Church *isn't* a matter of consumer-oriented, market-driven entertainment. It's God's idea, designed for our benefit.

> Church isn't a matter of consumer-oriented, market-driven entertainment. It's God's idea, designed for our benefit.

Jesus talked about the Christian church before it had even begun. And one of the main themes of the book of Acts, which tells the history of what Jesus' disciples did, is the setting up and organizing of local churches. The Apostle Paul spent his entire life setting up and helping local churches. The New Testament is made up primarily of letters written to churches and church leaders—letters that contain information about how we should behave in church, what church is for, and how we all can and should play a part. They teach about church membership, church discipline, church unity, and even the proper order for church services. They also talk about church leadership and list qualifications for church leaders. The book of James even warns about preferential seating in church meetings. The book of Hebrews tells us to submit to our church leaders and urges us to not stop meeting together. The last book of the Bible, Revelation, is also written to churches. With that focus, it's hard to read the New Testament without clearly understanding that church is God's idea.

But God didn't come up with this idea just to add more stress and responsibility to our lives. God invented church to help and benefit us. Church is a very important part of how life works and has far greater benefits than that extra hour of sleep, as research has shown.

Here's what *TIME* magazine said in a cover article titled "Faith and Healing: Can Spirituality Promote Health? Doctors Are Finding Some Surprising Evidence."

> Some scientists are beginning to look seriously at just what benefits patients may derive from spirituality. To their surprise, they are finding plenty of relevant data buried in the medical literature. More than 200 studies that touch on the role of religion have been ferreted out by [Dr. Jeffrey] Levin of Eastern Virginia and Dr. David Larson, a research psychiatrist formerly at the U.S. National Institutes of Health and now at the privately funded National Institute for Healthcare and Research. Most of these studies offer evidence that religion is good for one's health.
>
> Some highlights:

- A 1995 study at Dartmouth-Hitchcock Medical Center found that one of the best predictors of survival among 232 heart-surgery patients was the degree to which the patients said they drew comfort and strength from religious faith. Those who did not had more than three times the death rate of those who did.
- A survey of 30 years of research on blood pressure showed that churchgoers have lower blood pressure than nonchurchgoers—5 mm lower, according to Larson, even when adjusted to account for smoking and other risk factors.
- Other studies have shown that men and women who attend church regularly have half the risk of dying from coronary-artery disease as those who rarely go to church. Again, smoking and socioeconomic factors were taken into account.
- A 1996 National Institute on Aging study of 4,000 elderly living at home in North Carolina found that those who attend religious services are less depressed and physically healthier than those who don't attend or who worship at home.
- In a study of 30 female patients recovering from hip fractures, those who regarded God as a source of strength and comfort and who attended religious services were able to walk farther upon discharge and had lower rates of depression than those who had little faith.
- Numerous studies have found lower rates of depression and anxiety-related illness among the religiously committed. Nonchurchgoers have been found to have a suicide rate four times higher than church regulars.

There are many possible explanations for such findings. Since churchgoers are more apt than nonattendees to respect religious injunctions against drinking, drug abuse, smoking and other excesses, it's possible that their better health merely reflects these healthier habits.

Some of the studies, however, took pains to correct for

this possibility by making statistical adjustments for life-style differences. Larson likes to point out that in his own study the benefits of religion hold up strongly, even for those who indulge in cigarette smoking. Smokers who rated religion as being very important to them were one-seventh as likely to have an abnormal blood-pressure reading as smokers who did not value religion.

Churchgoing also offers social support—which numerous studies have shown to have a salutary effect on well-being. The Dartmouth heart-surgery study is one of the few that attempts to tease apart the effects of social support and religious conviction. Patients were asked separate sets of questions about their participation in social groups and the comfort they drew from faith. The two factors appeared to have distinct benefits that made for a powerful combination. Those who were both religious and socially involved had a 14-fold advantage over those who were isolated or lacked faith.[1]

It can't be said enough: church is God's idea. He gave it to us to provide many benefits to us and our children. Taking our children to church is an essential and powerful ingredient in raising our children in our faith. But in order to receive those benefits, we must understand the purpose behind the institution called *church*.

---

[1] *TIME*, June 24, 1996.

What's the purpose of church, and how can it help my children?

I TOOK A SURVEY AT SCHOOL AND FOUND OUT IF WE WOULD PUT IN A SWIMMING POOL, A BASKETBALL COURT AND COMPUTER TERMINALS WITH INTERACTIVE CHILDREN'S BIBLES, I COULD GET 98.7% OF THE KIDS TO COME.

If we want our children to adopt any life habit, life skill, or principle, we should explain to them why it's important and what the benefits are. Our job isn't done until they understand *why* we're asking them to do what we're asking them to do. The same goes for church. If we take or drag our children to church and never help them understand why, never help them see the purpose behind it, they'll find better things to do with their Sunday mornings when they're old enough to make the choice.

Three of the benefits church provides parents and children are help in the teaching process, support by a loving community, and opportunities for choosing and building good friendships.

Help in the Teaching Process

Life isn't lived in isolation, so it's very difficult to teach our children how to live and why a certain lifestyle is best unless they're involved in a larger group that supports and shares in the teaching process. This is one of the primary purposes for church in our children's lives: to help us in teaching our children about God and in preparing them for life. If we're the only ones involved in our children's spiritual life, the only ones who talk to them about God's principles and way of life, they may well end up thinking that anything that has to do with God is just our own personal hang-up.

Some people go to the other extreme. Many parents (and our culture in general) put the primary (or even sole) responsibility for teaching children spiritual matters on the church and its leaders. But it's impossible for pastors and Bible teachers to teach kids how to live God's way when they see them only one or two hours a week.

There isn't a single place in the Bible that puts this responsibility on the church. The primary task is ours, as parents, with the church there to assist and support us. The people who teach our children at church are delighted when we take an active role in spiritually training our children, and they will serve as active and effective advocates with us in that process.

> **There isn't a single place in the Bible that puts the responsibility for teaching children spiritual matters on the church.**

We need to help our children understand that one of the main reasons they go to church is to learn about God and his principles for life—knowledge that will help them be all that God wants them to be and have a good, rewarding life. It's fine to talk to them about all the fun they'll have, but we need to encourage them with the benefits of learning as well. (It's not unlike school. Although kids know that school can be fun and that they can spend time with their friends there, they also understand that the primary purpose of school is for them to learn and to gain the benefits of an education.)

Incidentally, this learning angle will help you when your children become bored with church and don't want to go. If the only reason for going is to have fun, and they're not *having* fun, you have nothing left to motivate them with. But if one of the primary reasons for church attendance is for them to learn, then you can continue to motivate them to go, even as you seek ways of making the experience more enjoyable.

Some helpful tips:

- On the way to church talk briefly about how you're looking forward to learning more about God during the service and study hour and suggest how that knowledge will help you. On the way home briefly mention what you learned and get your children talking about what they did, what fun they had, what songs they sang, and what their Bible story or Bible lesson was about. This will help to reinforce what your children learned. Try not to add your own lengthy sermon to what they say the lesson was; instead, be excited about it and praise them for what they're learning.
- Talk to your children's teachers and find out what they're teaching. Talk to your children too, and help them with their lessons—just as you'd help them with their homework and talk to them about what they're learning at school. Help them to understand and memorize their memory verses, for example, and review during the week the Bible story or Bible passage they focused on the previous Sunday at church. If they learned a specific life principle, look for opportunities to encourage them in an upbeat way to apply what they learned, emphasizing the benefits of doing so.
- Be sure, however, to make church not *merely* a learning process. Make it fun as well. If your church meets in the morning, take your children out to lunch afterward or prepare their favorite foods for lunch at home. Make

Sunday afternoon special, with the purpose of having your children always look forward to "church day." Try to make the process of getting ready and traveling to and from church a positive one. If you're tired or not looking forward to going yourself, try to keep your whining muffled. If after church you're struggling with something someone said or you feel that you got less than nothing out of church that day, bite your tongue. Any negative comments you make will come back to haunt you in the future, disguised as the reasons your children want to stay home. Don't misunderstand: I'm not saying that we should always paste on smiles and pretend that our church is perfect. I'm saying that we should save our comments and discussions about problems until a time when our kids are old enough to understand them in a broader context. (It's like the problems that sometimes come up in a good marriage: you don't discuss them in front of or with the kids until they're old enough to understand the difference between a minor issue and a major crisis.)

• When your church schedules something fun and extra—a field trip, a party, a play, a midweek kids' club, or anything else your children would enjoy or ask to attend—make it a priority to get them there. Look for any and every opportunity to make church an enjoyable experience. Help them stay excited about it.

Support by a Loving Community

The second purpose and benefit church provides is community. When we bring our children up with the support of a loving Christian community, our children are encouraged by others, inspired by their example, and held accountable by a wider group than just their own parents. In addition, we as parents are supported and helped in our task of parenting.

Jesus himself grew up in community and benefited from it:

Every years Jesus' parents went to Jerusalem for the Passover Feast. When he was 12 years old, they went up to the Feast as usual.

After the Feast was over, his parents left to go back home. The boy Jesus stayed behind in Jerusalem. But they were not aware of it. They thought he was somewhere in their group. So they traveled on for a day.

Then they began to look for him among their relatives and friends. They did not find him. So they went back to Jerusalem to look for him.

(LUKE 2:42–45)

Sometimes when we think of Jesus' childhood we picture an incredibly wise and aloof boy who spent his time alone, studying, thinking, and praying—probably pretty much a loner except when he took a break to teach one of the other kids something important. Not so! The biblical passage above tells us that Jesus' parents were so accustomed to Jesus' being with friends and relatives in his community that they didn't even notice that he wasn't with them on their journey until they'd been traveling for an entire day! Another Bible verse that talks about Jesus' childhood says that Jesus "grew in wisdom and stature and in favor with God and man." In other words, he got more and more well liked (not as someone special but as a regular kid) in his community as he grew up. So much so that later, when he was an adult, his popularity stopped him from effectively talking to and helping the people in his own hometown; because they'd known and liked him all his life, they had trouble seeing him as the Messiah.

Our children need to be around other people and learn from them. They need to see people other than their parents living God's way. They need to know mentors at every stage of life who teach by living, struggling, and succeeding where our kids can see them—family friends, relatives, colleagues, regular people doing their best to live God's way, leaders, counselors, Bible teachers, volunteers, people in businesses or careers that our kids are considering. There should be a whole range of people of different ages painting pictures with their lives, words, and actions for our children to store in their memories and draw on in daily life. Jesus taught by using stories and parables about farmers, tax collectors, priests, businessmen, merchants, tradesmen, the poor, the rich, widows, and many more—a gallery of real-life people from his community teaching real-life lessons.

What do we mean by *community*? In Jesus' day community was limited to the people in one's hometown: family, friends, and faith were all in one location. Today, although community is still defined to some extent by location, the distance someone can live from us and still be an active part of our lives and community is a whole lot greater than walking distance. Our family's community today is defined by the people we live with as well as the people we spend time with on a regular basis, regardless of distance. Although our community involves everyone in our family members' daily lives, the core should be those who will help, support, and grow with us in our faith—and that's where our churches come in.

Someone once said that who you are five years from now will depend on the people you spend your time with and the books you read. We're all taught, influenced, and mentored, whether intentionally or not, by the people we spend time with and by the information we feed our hearts and minds. With today's ease of communication and transportation, we're involved in and flitting between so many relationships and social/work/school groups that we lose the benefits of any kind of stable, ongoing community. Friendship, accountability, personal growth, community spirit, mentoring, caring, and support can all be lost. Today more than at any other time in history, true community doesn't happen naturally; we must choose to *make* it happen. It's important for us to focus on building a strong faith community for our families and children, since the technology that allows us to widen our community can also cause us to lose it.

One of the most powerful benefits for our kids of being part of a strong community is that they can see and learn from youth who are slightly older then they are. *Youthviews,* a newsletter published by the Gallup organization, reported these statistics:

- 57% of teens said they'd like to help other teens with both their schoolwork and their personal problems; in other words, they'd like to tutor as well as mentor those younger than themselves.
- 35% of all teens said they'd enjoyed being mentored at one point in their lives.
- Of those teens surveyed who said they'd never been tutored or mentored, some 33% expressed interest in getting help academically while another 28% expressed interest in getting help with personal problems.[2]

We all know that our children look up to those in the next age group, and we get nervous about it because we think that those older kids may be involved in things that we don't want our kids involved in. Our concern is understandable, yet community mentoring is the system God created. It's natural for kids to look up to those who are older, and the next age group can be of enormous benefit to our children. They can learn from the example of the older group and take the next step in wisdom and responsibility, the next step in life. Church involvement provides a kind of peer pressure for good rather than evil. When our children grow up in a good church community where the

> **Our children need to be around other people and learn from them—a whole range of people of different ages painting pictures with their lives, words, and actions for our children to store in their memories and draw on in daily life.**

[2]*Youthviews: The Newsletter of the Gallup Youth Survey* (Princeton, N.J.: George H. Gallup International Institute), vol. 3, no. 8 (Apr. 1996).

other children are being taught God's principles for life, we can be excited by, instead of nervous about, mentoring.

Some helpful tips:

- Building a loving church community for our children takes more than just finding and/or attending a local church and showing up for an hour or two once a week. The church we choose (if we don't have one already) should ideally already have a small part of our friendship community involved in it. For example, if some of our relatives, friends, people we work with, classmates, or neighbors attend a particular church, that church would be a great place for us to take our family, because we already have a community foundation on which we can build. From there we can begin to get involved, take part, meet more people, and build ourselves into a Christian community.

- If you don't have a church where you already know some people, the best thing to do is to choose a church where building community will not be difficult. For example, a church that's in or close to your neighborhood will likely have members who live in your area. (Being part of the same geographical community will help in establishing personal community.) If you were raised in, or have some history with, a particular brand of Christian church, choosing the same denomination will give you some common ground when meeting church members. Look for a place that has a fair number of families at the same stage of life, who have children around the same ages as yours.

- We shouldn't look for the perfect church—we'd spoil it by joining. The church is supposed to be a place where we can feel free to share our joys as well as our hurts and our failings, knowing that we won't be judged or rejected but rather supported and embraced. God's church is a place where saints as well as sinners belong. A faith community is made up of people—*regular* people. We shouldn't expect it to be perfect, only caring and growing.

- Don't be afraid to visit and ask questions. Most churches welcome visitors. After a few visits and a round or two of questions and answers, discuss with your family how they feel about the church, whether they think they could find friends there and fit in, and whether they feel "at home" there. If your family participates in finding a church, it will be easier to promote family participation afterward.

- Take some time and put some prayer, thought, and discussion into this decision. It takes time to build your family into a faith community, and taking some extra time up front is much better than moving to a different church after a few months or years of disappointment and having to start all over again.

If you're already involved in a church and have a sense of community there, begin to get involved in more than just the Sunday morning service; make an effort to get to know others and to actively build community. Take your children to the activities that are planned for them, and if possible get involved in the organizing of such activities—not just the fun events but also educational and charitable activities. We often shy away from volunteering and seeking greater involvement because we're so busy already, but if we realized the benefits and pleasures of being part of a growing, supporting, loving community, we'd run to get involved. It takes time and effort to build a faith-centered community for your family, but the long-term effects and rewards are worth the effort.

Opportunities for Choosing and Building Good Friendships

Anyone who walks with wise people grows wise.
But a companion of foolish people suffers harm.

(PROVERBS 13:20)

Don't let anyone fool you. "Bad companions make good persons bad."

(1 CORINTHIANS 15:33)

Probably the most concrete benefit of church is that our
children grow up with and choose as their primary friends
those who are also learning about God.

Youthviews reported these statistics on peer pressure:

- 19% of teens said that they feel a great deal of pressure to
  party whether they want to or not; another 30%—a fairly
  significant figure—said that they feel pressure some of
  the time.
- 9% of teens said that they experience a lot of pressure to
  have sexual relationships; 27% said that they regularly
  experience pressure to do so.
- 7% of teens said that they feel a great deal of pressure to
  drink; 21% said that they feel some pressure.
- 7% of teens said that they feel a lot of pressure to smoke
  marijuana; 13% said that they feel some pressure.[3]

Can we control who our children choose as friends? Yes
and no. We may not be able to choose their friends for them,
but we *can* control to a large extent which "menu" their
friends will be chosen from. If our family is going out for dinner and we're concerned about the type of food that our children eat, we'll choose a restaurant that has a menu with the
right kind of food on it. It would be silly to take our kids to
fast-food places every time we eat out and then wonder why
they're always eating junk food.

Likewise, we can choose the community our children
choose their friends from. When we purposely establish a
faith community for our children and actively get them

---

[3]Ibid.

involved, we're presenting them with the healthiest possible menu of friends.

Some helpful tips:

- Most kids have more than one menu to choose from—church, school, and neighborhood, for example—but there are ways in which parents can help children choose from the right menu. Whenever possible, say yes to all activities and outings that involve the right menu, and make an effort to get your children there. In advance, suggest and help plan visits, events, and activities with the right group of friends. (This will keep you way ahead of the game, since our children's plans are usually last-minute.) Schedule your family in advance to be involved in any activities that are being sponsored by your church. Your children will develop friendships with the people they're with most often. You can also make a point of getting to know the parents of these children and arrange visits as families.

- It's much easier to steer positively in the right direction than to try to make a midcourse correction. It's far more effective to direct our children's community than it is to try to correct their friendships. Spending our time trying to break up friendships or telling our children that they can't spend time with kids that they already know and like is generally counterproductive. If your children currently have friendships you'd like to end, don't attack the friendships or the friends; simply start building your children's community in a more positive direction and allow the friendships to change in the process.

- This process may sound sneaky, but it isn't—if we let our children know what we're doing. They need to understand how friendships can affect them and how important it is to choose good friends. Talk to them about these things and tell them how you plan on helping them have the best possible friends to choose from. Helping our children understand the process will make our job a whole lot easier.

- When attempting to steer your children away from existing friendships toward healthier ones, be careful not to
  tell them that they can't be with their old friends any
  longer. Once they understand the benefits of choosing
  and spending time with the right friends, help them
  understand that it's not that they can't see or talk to their
  old friends; rather, they need to spend more of their time
  with friends who share their own values and goals. Help
  them understand the difference between casual friendships and close friendships. We should be friendly,
  respectful, and accepting of everyone, but we should
  choose our close friends—the ones we want to share our
  lives and hearts with—from people who share the same
  life goals and heart focus.

I

sn't there a right and a wrong way for a church to believe and teach? Is it important to take my children to a certain church?

Christian churches come in a wider assortment of flavors than jelly beans. If we were to take a tour of all the different churches, we'd find church leaders dressed in robes, in suits, and in jeans. We'd hear music ranging from traditional hymns to upbeat choruses and from rock and roll to country. Some of the music would be accompanied by clapping hands and dancing feet, some by a hushed stillness. We'd visit very traditional services where the minister's words and the congregation's responses were scripted, and we'd visit very unstructured gatherings where everyone contributed to the service as the Spirit moved them—as well as everything between these two extremes. We'd sit through forty-five-minute services with ten-minute sermons and two-and-a-half-hour services with seventy-five-minute sermons. We'd find churches where everyone dressed in black and technology wasn't invited and televised services that featured professional entertainment. We'd find church services held in the living room of someone's home and high-tech services staged in multi-million-dollar structures that seat tens of thousands.

We'd walk into churches that followed hundreds of years of history and tradition, churches grounded in the history of a particular denomination, and churches based on the religious traditions of other countries or cultures around the world. Then we'd worship in churches only a few years old that were in the process of defining their own traditions based only on the existing culture.

We'd also find that although all these churches taught the same basics, each one had a slightly different emphasis in its message. One church would stress holy living, another would emphasize prayer and opening our hearts to God, another would focus on the message of salvation through the cross, and still another would stress God's blessings.

Given this incredible variety, which church has it right? Each church believes that its own way of doing things is very important, and that's as it should be; but when we look at things from the outside and see all the ways in which churches express their faith, it begins to seem like the difference between apple pie and pumpkin pie at Thanksgiving—a matter of taste.

When Jesus said, "I am the way and the truth and the life. No one comes to the Father except through me" (John 14:6), he wasn't trying to start an exclusive club of people who think, act, live, and express themselves in one singular and particular way. The exact opposite is the truth.

But that's not all there is to it. God created the potential for vast variety and creativity in the forms of expression his children favor. He doesn't want us all to be cookie-cutter Christians in the way in which we express and celebrate our relationship with him.

When Jesus said, "I am the way and the truth and the life. No one comes to the Father except through me" (John 14:6), he wasn't trying to start an exclusive club of people who think, act, live, and express themselves in one singular and particular way. The exact opposite is the truth. Jesus was stating one—and only one—requirement for admission in order to keep it simple; he opened heaven's doors to all people and all cultures with all their differences and in all their variety.

God's attitude toward church is kind of like that of parents who give their children paint, canvas, and paintbrushes and show them how to paint—and then allow them to develop their own painting instead of insisting that they paint by numbers or imitate others. As a result, the potential for variety in cultural, traditional, and individual church expression and emphasis is limitless.

Does that mean that it doesn't make any difference what we do or believe? Not at all. But it's critically important that we separate for our children the *essentials* of our faith from the way we *express* and *celebrate* our faith. All Christian churches agree on the basics of faith as outlined in the Apostles' Creed, a statement of the essentials of the faith dating in its earliest form to the first three centuries of the church.

The Apostles' Creed

We believe in God, the Father Almighty,
*   maker of heaven and earth;*
And in Jesus Christ his only Son, our Lord;
*   who was conceived by the Holy Spirit,*
*   born of the Virgin Mary,*
*   suffered under Pontius Pilate,*
*   was crucified, dead, and buried;*
*   he descended into hades;*
*   the third day he rose again from the dead;*
*   he ascended into heaven,*
*   and sits on the right hand of God, the Father Almighty;*
*   from there he shall come to judge the living and the dead.*

We believe in the Holy Spirit,
     the holy Christian church,
     the communion of saints,
     the forgiveness of sins,
     the resurrection of the body,
     and the life everlasting.
Amen.

These are the things that all Christian churches *agree* on and that form the foundation of our faith. The things that *vary* from Christian church to Christian church fall into three broad categories:

1. The way in which we express our faith, which is affected by our culture and the history and traditions of each particular church.
2. The emphasis or flavor of the message, which also has a lot to do with the history of that church and the needs of the community or culture that the church is in.
3. The way in which secondary issues and/or doctrines are viewed. For example, some churches may talk a lot about divine healing—which isn't a core doctrine of the historic church or a prerequisite to faith in God; rather, it's what the Psalmist would call a "benefit"—while other churches take the stand that healing isn't something we should teach about.

If we explain these things to our children—what's essential to our faith and what's more a matter of taste—we can avoid some basic problems later on. The benefits to helping our children understand the distinction between what's essential and what's a matter of preference are many:

• First, young people sooner or later realize that there is a wide variety of churches and ways of expressing our faith. If they've been brought up believing that Christianity is right but have also been taught or have

adopted the attitude that their particular way of expressing it is the *only* correct way, then, as they get older and
begin to question things, they may well confuse question-
ing the form in which their faith is expressed with ques-
tioning their faith in God—and they may end up rejecting
both. But if they understand that all of these Christian
churches hold to the essentials of the faith—essentials
that are true—then exploring the way other churches
do and view things will strengthen rather than weaken
their faith.

- Second, helping our children understand these things will
cause them to be more accepting and understanding of
the larger Christian family and of members of that family
who do things differently than they're used to.

- Third, our children will understand the difference
between a Christian church and pseudo-Christian cults
that may approach them later in their lives. The primary
thing that separates a Christian church from a cult
(besides the spaceship hiding behind the comet) is that a
cult claims new revelation and denies and/or strays from
the basics of the Christian faith. And to cover up this fun-
damental discrepancy, a cult claims to be the only group
that knows the *real* truth.

- Finally, our children will understand that, beyond the
basics of Christianity, their faith isn't so much about what
they believe about secondary issues or how they express
their faith; rather, it's about knowing God—and about
who they become and how they live as a result of that
relationship.

A balancing comment must be made here. The ways in
which we express our faith and the beauty and richness of
our church traditions are extensions of our past and can be
beautiful expressions of who we are and how we relate to
God as a church community. It's important to separate what's
essential from what's secondary—but that doesn't mean that
we should try to eliminate or in any way denigrate the forms

in which we express our faith, whether they be liturgical or contemporary. Probably the best way to preserve our traditions is to help our children enjoy them and benefit from them. We can do this by teaching our traditions as a beautiful way of expressing our faith and by helping our kids understand why we do them and what they mean.

> It's important to separate what's essential from what's secondary—but that doesn't mean that we should try to eliminate or in any way denigrate the forms in which we express our faith, whether they be liturgical or contemporary.

If you're curious as to whether a church that you or your children have visited is a *Christian* church, ask for a copy of its statement of faith. Every church should have one and will be glad to supply you with a copy. See if the basics line up with the creed above. This exercise will also give you an opportunity to read between the lines and see what the church's emphasis is and what its position is on some of the secondary issues. These two things—primary emphasis and stance on secondary issues—shouldn't be the main consideration when you're making your decision about a church; nonetheless, your personal comfort level and your ability to build community will be enhanced if the church you choose views things as you do.

My spouse and I come from different church backgrounds. How can we agree on where to take the children to church?

We all tend to fall back on what we know and have experienced. If we were raised to express our faith in a certain way, it's understandable that we would feel more comfortable taking our children to the same kind of church. Yet we often have unpleasant memories connected with that same familiar church experience—the experience that we now want to put our children through. When it comes to deciding which church to attend as a family, your children should come ahead of the "but that's the church I went to" consideration if you want to make the church experience a positive one that will last them a lifetime.

The best way to begin to resolve the problem of different church backgrounds is to sit down with your spouse and go over a list of what's important in a church for your family. Here are some of the things you should consider:

- One of the primary purposes for taking children to church is to have the church help in the spiritual teaching process. We therefore need to find a church that has good Bible classes and programs and that's diligent about teaching kids—not a church that merely baby-sits or entertains kids. After visiting a church, ask your children what they did and what they learned. Look in the church bulletin or on the bulletin board to see what kind of Sunday morning and midweek programs are available for children and youth.

- Another important aspect of church that we've already discussed is community. Churches of the denominations that you and your spouse were raised in may be located across town, and you may not know a single person who attends either of them. Yet there may be a Christian church of a different flavor just a few blocks away, attended by several of your friends and/or neighbors and some children your kids go to school with. This church is worthy of strong consideration, because the seeds that will help you begin to build community are already there.

- Try to list things that both of you liked about the churches you grew up in. You may be able to find these same elements in a church with a different label. For example, you may like a traditional format for a service, while your spouse may dislike hymns and want music that's contemporary; you may be looking for a church with a midweek girls' and boys' club, while your spouse may feel strongly about how the church baptizes people.

Once you've finished separating the elements of church that are important to each of you from the actual church you were raised in, visit some local churches. After you've sampled a few, pick one with good programs for your kids, seeds of community, other people in your demographic pattern, and some of the important considerations on both of your lists. And don't forget to involve the children in your decision. After visiting each church, find out what they think. The church you choose may end up being a church from one of your backgrounds or a completely new one, but you'll have arrived at the decision as a family, and you'll all know why you're worshiping there.

Another important detail—talk to God and ask him to give you wisdom in the process and help you find the right place. He knows where your family will fit best.

W

hat about special services for children, such as baptism, dedication, and confirmation? Are these an important part of my children's spiritual development?

DOES YOUR CHURCH HAVE CHRISTENING, BAPTISM, DEDICATION AND CONFIRMATION? YOU KNOW, IN A PACKAGE DEAL? I WANT TO MAKE SURE THAT I DON'T MISS ANYTHING IMPORTANT.

Picture this scene. After many months of loving labor, working with your daughter and meticulously planning every glorious detail of her wedding, you've just been rewarded with one of the most beautiful experiences of your life. The wedding was very expensive, but everything was spectacular, magazine-spread-perfect, and incredibly moving. Your daughter is now about to embark on the next stage of her life. Tears of joy and a few tears of sadness mix in an emotional stream as you run out to the front of the church to say good-bye. As you release your newlywed daughter from your loving embrace, sending her to her husband with your blessing, an unfamiliar car pulls up to the curb. After a quick wave, the husband throws his luggage in the back and slips into the passenger seat next to some girl you've never met.

Your daughter, seeing the shock and confusion on your face, comforts you with these words: "Oh, don't worry; it's cool with me. Just because we got married doesn't mean we're going to do that 'husband and wife' thing! But we really wanted that wedding ceremony, and it was awesome! Do you want to go get some pizza?" It doesn't take a lot of imagination to know what the nature and tone of the conversation would be over the pizza.

Getting married isn't just about having a great service. A wedding is a ceremony that celebrates a mutual commitment to love each other and to work at the shared life that that commitment will bring. There's no special magic involved in a wedding ceremony that somehow prepares the participants for what lies ahead or guarantees the successful honoring of the commitment or the success of the marriage.

Any ceremony involving the baptism, dedication, or confirmation of a baby or a child is also a ceremony of commitment and a celebration of what that commitment means and brings. And as with a wedding, it shouldn't be a ceremony simply for the sake of ceremony. The ceremony alone confers no special magic guaranteeing that your child will lead a spiritual life full of God's blessing.

When it comes to the baptism, dedication, or confirmation of a baby or a child, churches vary in their beliefs and practices. The reason for this variety is that there isn't a place in the Bible that sets forward a clear, concise, and exact pattern as to how these occasions are to be handled. The Bible verses and biblical examples that are used to support the baptism, dedication, and confirmation of young people don't conclude with commandments or give specific instructions. Therefore, much of the variation comes down to the different ways, historically and traditionally, through which different churches express their faith in this area. One issue that most everyone agrees on, however, is the main purpose and motivation behind these varied ceremonies: commitment.

All ceremonies involving the dedication, baptism, or confirmation of a baby or a child fall into one of two categories. The first category involves babies and/or very young children and centers around the parents' commitment: the parents commit the child to God and commit before God to bring the child up in the Christian faith. The second involves older children and is centered around a commitment from them to live God's way.

Any ceremony of commitment requires thought and preparation. If you want to participate in a ceremony to commit your young ones to God and commit yourself to bringing them up God's way, you need to understand what the ceremony means, what you're committing to, and what the commitment involves. Some churches provide classes for parents in preparation for such ceremonies. Churches that don't offer formal preparation often provide relevant literature and the opportunity for discussion with church leaders.

If your older children want to be involved in a ceremony of commitment, join with them in striving to understand the ceremony and its implications and help them prepare for it. If they're going through classes, help them understand what they're learning and what that knowledge will mean to their lives.

If you're in a church where a confirmation ceremony automatically happens at a certain age or after passing a certain class or catechism, help your children understand that this is more than a ritual and involves a commitment to God. Let them know that they should go through with the ceremony only if they truly want to make the commitment.

Be sure to make any and all ceremonies and services of this kind memorable and beautiful occasions for yourself and for your children. They're not only ceremonies of commitment; like weddings, they're also celebrations of the wonderful things that commitment will bring.

4.

Prayer

~~~~~~~~~~~~~~~~~~~~~~~~~~~~~~~~~~~~~

A. How can I explain to my children what prayer is?

B. How important is it for my children to kneel and fold their hands and close their eyes?

C. How can I help my children's prayers grow *with* them so that they don't grow *out* of them?

D. What things should I be encouraging my children to pray about?

E. Are memorized prayers important, and are they effective?

F. How do I explain things to my children when their prayers aren't answered?

~~~~~~~~~~~~~~~~~~~~~~~~~~~~~~~~~~~~~

How can I explain to my children what prayer is?

Polls conducted in North America by various groups over the last five years show that there's a surprising amount of prayer going on.

- 88% of us pray.
- 78% describe prayer as an important part of daily life.
- 63% pray often.
- 25% pray occasionally.
- 65% believe that they've had specific answers to prayer.
- 79% believe that praying helps speed physical recovery.
- 24% believe that they've been cured through prayer.[1]

An amazing thing about prayer is how universal it is. It seems to be a natural response and activity of the human heart. No matter where you search in the world or in history, it's impossible to find a society that doesn't have some concept of prayer.

God created us as his children, and since our relationship with him was intended to be not merely a great and wonderful part of our lives but the very foundation on which we would grow, learn, and accomplish, he wired us for prayer. He not only created us with all the built-in hardware and software for communication with him, so that we could talk with him on a regular basis, but he also created all of life to work in harmony with prayer.

> In recent years, scientific and medical research has begun to show that prayer makes a distinct difference in our mental and physical health and in our lives in general.

In recent years, scientific and medical research has begun to investigate prayer and its effects. The majority of the results show that prayer makes a distinct difference in our mental and physical health and in our lives in general. Magazine articles, books, and reports of all types are being published on the topic. One study that received a lot of attention was conducted in 1988 by cardiologist Randolph Byrd at San Francisco General Hospital. Although some have questioned the validity of the study because of the way it was designed, the results were significant enough to make them hard to doubt. In fact, if similar results had been achieved while studying a new medical treatment, the treatment would have been called a medical breakthrough.

---

[1]Summary report of faith in America provided for Lightwave Publishing by Roper Center of Conn. (Storrs, Conn.), 1997. That report cites findings from the following: The *Washington Post*, with interviewing conducted by ICR Survey Research Group, July 19, 1997; surveys by *Time*/CNN/Yankelovich Partners, January 13, 1995, and June 25, 1996; CBS News/*New York Times* Poll, September 18–22, 1995; Princeton Research Associates, September 21, 1994.

The study randomly divided 393 patients from the coronary-care unit into two groups. One group was prayed for by Christians; the other was not. Neither group was told of the experiment. The results? The group that was prayed for had far less need for medication and/or medical treatment than the group that went without prayer. The prayed-for group also had improved overall health. And the only difference was prayer; the patients' expectations couldn't affect the outcome since none of them knew that anyone was being prayed for.

> **Prayer is a natural part of who we are and how we were created, and it's part of the structure that makes our lives work.**

Many of the scientists involved in this and other studies on the effects of prayer, as well as those who merely look on, have tried to find physiological and natural explanations for why people who pray and are prayed for seem to be healthier and happier than those without prayer. Prayer seems to have an effect on various parts of the brain and the body—inducing relaxation, encouraging a positive mental outlook, and reducing stress—but the big question is why?

Many of the researchers have concluded that the physiological or psychological benefits of prayer are the result of natural processes, that prayer has nothing to do with God but only with nature. Of course, that's the only conclusion you *can* come to if you don't believe that there's a God who answers prayer. In actuality, with each new study and each new research finding, scientists are proving more certainly that God designed every part of us and life itself to function and work by and with prayer.

God created everything in harmony with the foundational idea of our communicating with him as our Father, and these studies show the incredible intricacy and unity of God's design. Prayer is a natural part of who we are and how we were created, and it's part of the structure that makes our lives work.

Over the years, the whole idea of prayer and what prayer is and does has gotten complicated and confused. As society's ideas of who God is were "fuzzified," so were our ideas about prayer. If we want to teach our children about prayer—what it is and how to go about it—we need to bring it back to its most basic and simple level: prayer is talking with God, just as conversation is communicating with other people.

Prayer isn't a goal unto itself, or a religious activity that we do to get on God's good side. Prayer is simply talking and communicating with our loving Heavenly Father, who wants to teach us, guide us, provide for us, protect us, care for us, and help us have a full life and be all that he created us to be. We must be careful that we don't teach our children about prayer as if it were some mysterious activity. It should be no more complicated for them than communicating with us as their parents.

How important is it for my children to kneel and fold their hands and close their eyes?

AND THANK YOU GOD FOR DANCING FEET AND THE FOOD WE'RE ABOUT TO EAT!

There's no magic in the position we choose for prayer or in what we do with our hands or eyes. We find in the Bible examples of people praying in various positions and postures and in various places.

Position

The Bible tells of people praying in a variety of different positions. Daniel knelt, Elijah put his head between his knees, Solomon raised his hands, David danced, and Moses either stood or lay down flat on his face. None of these positions was required; in each case the position was chosen by the person praying and reflected his attitude or mood.

Whatever position your children prefer to pray in is appropriate, whether it be lying in bed, sitting in a comfortable chair, kneeling, or some other posture. But you can help your children understand that sometimes

> We need to bring prayer back to its most basic and simple level: prayer is talking with God, just as conversation is communicating with other people.

it's good to choose a different position for their prayers. For example, if they say their prayers lying in bed at night and keep falling asleep in the middle of praying, perhaps a less comfortable position would help their concentration. (Remind them that God is there with them, and he really is listening. Would they consider falling asleep while talking with one of their friends?) You can also let your children know that it's perfectly fine to change position while praying, depending on what they're talking to God about. For example, they may usually pray lying down, but if they have something special and serious they want to talk to God about, they might want to get on their knees beside the bed.

The same is true of what we do with our hands. If your children are fidgeting when they should be concentrating,

> The more time we spend with God, concentrating on him and communicating with him, the more real he'll be to us.

they may find that clasping their hands helps them focus, but there's no single prescribed way for holding our hands in prayer.

Having eyes open or closed while praying is a more significant issue. Although there's no biblical mandate to close our eyes, closed eyes are for most people more conducive to prayer. It's considered polite to look at someone we're in conversation with, as an indication that we're interested and listening. That suggests *open* eyes—but not when the conversation is with God. When we're talking to God we obviously can't see him with our eyes, but we know he's present when we pray and can be seen with our hearts. You can explain to your children that in order to show God that we're interested and concentrating, we should close our eyes so that we can focus on him with our hearts, our thoughts, and our feelings. The more time we spend with God, concentrating on him and communicating with him, the more real he'll be to us, visible to our hearts.

Time and Location

We need to reinforce with our children the fact of God's continual presence. He's always there, wherever we are, always listening, and always ready to help. We can teach our children about three ways in which they can talk with God during the day:

- *Anytime prayers* are prayed whenever your children think of something they want to talk to God about or thank him for, no matter where they are or what they're doing. You should encourage your kids to use anytime prayers frequently so that their relationship with God isn't something thrown in as an afterthought before they go to sleep at night. It's a good idea to offer such prayers yourself, with your children, when you think of someone or something to pray about. Briefly let them know what you're thinking of talking to God about and then informally and naturally and briefly pray the prayer and go on with what you were doing—all without missing a beat.
- *Important-moment prayers* are prayed on the spot when something important happens to your children or they're faced with some kind of emergency. Encourage your kids to make prayer their first response to urgent situations— if someone at their school gets hurt, or there's an altercation, or they or someone else is in some kind of trouble, for example. This is an important aspect of prayer for children, because they live in the moment. At the end of the day, before going to bed, they may find it hard to think back and remember all the things they might have

wanted to talk to God about. Again, this is something you can do with your children when the occasion arises. Remember to keep prayer simple and normal, though, whether you're doing the praying or your kids are. Lowering your voice a few notches, talking in solemn tones, or using words or language you don't use in every-day speech tells your children that prayer is something that isn't part of everyday life. It also sends the wrong message to them about how real God is and how he understands and relates to them.

- *Time-with-God prayers* should be offered by our children at a regular time every day. Help your children under-stand that if they have friends and want to get to know them better, they can't just say hello when they pass them in the hall or talk to them in a group. If they really want to get close as friends, they need to spend time together. In the same way, our children need to set aside time daily to build this most important and most foundational rela-tionship of all—with God.

With your younger children the best time for this prayer is before bed and after story time and Bible story time. Your older children should be able to change this time if they'd rather do something else before going to bed. But it's impor-tant that you help your children develop a daily habit of set-aside time for prayer. This should become a priority, right up there with taking a bath, dressing, and brushing teeth. Actually, it should be at the very top of the list, since prayer has by far the greatest impact on their lives. But it's good for kids to learn to look at prayer as a natural part of everyday life. They wouldn't go to school in the morning without brushing or combing their hair, and they wouldn't consider missing breakfast, lunch, or dinner. Neither should they con-sider missing their prayer time.

How can I help my children's prayers grow *with* them so that they don't grow *out* of them?

The training process for almost everything we teach our children is progressive. We start at ground zero, progress step by step, and end up with young people who are fully prepared to tackle life on their own. The same sequence is true for prayer. We need to start talking to our children about, and walking them through, the basics of prayer when they're still very young. We can then move them progressively forward so that when they leave our care they have a strong, healthy, and growing prayer life.

We talked earlier in the book about a basic parenting principle: when teaching your kids something, explain the process to them and help them understand it so that they can begin to take ownership of the goal and be motivated in the training process. Our children should know what their prayer life should look like when they leave home. They should also know what the intermediate goals are as we move them progressively along. One of the main reasons we lose our children in any life-training process is that we take them to a certain level and then stop, expecting them to take over at that point. But they can't travel without someone's help if they don't know where they're going, why they're headed that direction, and how exactly to get there. Therefore, any training process must continue until it's complete.

As we proceed through the prayer training process, we need to remember that each one of our children is unique, and that no effective training can follow a cookie-cutter pattern. The general stages and ideas outlined in this section should be used as a general guide in the process, but they should be used with flexibility to allow for our children's responses and growth. We shouldn't try to force our children to fit into the exact mold of a heavily regimented training process.

On the contrary, we should reinforce and celebrate our children's uniqueness. God didn't create any of us alike, and he responds to each one of us as individuals. God created for each one of our children a special opportunity for a relationship with him that can never be duplicated. God loves our children uniquely and wants a special relationship with them that no one else can step into. Telling our children this will help them understand—even more as they grow older—that prayer isn't a religious *exercise* that we perform. It's an individual and very real relationship with our wonderful, loving Father.

Praying with Babies

When our children are barely old enough to understand what we're saying, we should begin to pray with them each night before putting them to sleep—briefly, and in simple, clear language. We should pray their prayers for them, not our prayers over them. We might start out with something as simple as thanking God for something special about our child's day and asking him to help the child have a good sleep.

As our children begin to talk and take an interest in different things, we should keep our prayers short and change our prayers regularly to reflect what's going on in our children's lives, the things they're interested in. When our children are old enough to begin to understand, we can tell them each night what we're doing: that we're talking to God, who made them and loves them and wants to take care of them.

> God loves our children uniquely and wants a special relationship with them that no one else can step into.

Praying with Toddlers

At this stage of our children's growth we should probably continue to say their prayers for them. But we need to begin to teach them that this is *their* prayer time, not ours. We can spend a few more minutes praying with them and help them to close their eyes, to be still, and to concentrate on God, who is listening and loves them.

If you need help motivating your children to be still, try putting a little active play time in the schedule. That way you can help them be still by letting them look forward to the play time that comes next. Or if your children get a snack or drink before bed that they look forward to, put it right after prayer in the routine; then they'll be motivated to concentrate on prayer so that they can get to their snack. Don't worry about some restlessness; praise them and reward them when they're still, and continue to encourage them by telling them how much God loves them and wants to hear from them. The concentration will come eventually. Prayer time isn't a very good time to get all bent out of shape about discipline and about having your children respond to you perfectly. If prayer time becomes a battle, it will be hard for you to help your children look forward to it and want to learn more about it.

At this stage we should pray about things that emphasize

God's care and love. Probably around the time our children are four or five years old, we can begin to involve them in deciding what we're going to pray for them. This confirms to them that these are *their* prayers and that eventually, as they get bigger, they'll say them for themselves—the you're-getting-bigger-and-growing-up motivation. We can ask them what they'd like to pray about, giving them some suggestions from things that we know are currently of interest to them, things that happened that day, special events that are coming up, or events scheduled for the next day. Once they've agreed to one or two items, we should pray simply and briefly, again using words they'd use themselves, keeping the prayer upbeat and praising them for thinking of good things to pray about.

Praying with Kids Just Starting School

At this next stage, after deciding together what should be prayed, we can have our children repeat the prayers after us. Again remembering that each child is an individual, we may find that some of our children want to and are ready to start saying their own prayers at this point. We should also be reinforcing the basics of how God wants to teach us and care for us and give us the best possible life, pointing out that one way we receive this care is by prayer, by talking to God about our lives. As in each one of these prayer stages, we should let our children know ahead of time that in a matter of weeks or after their next birthday (or at some other milestone of our choosing), they'll be bigger and it will be time to graduate to the next prayer step; and we should explain what that next step will be.

Praying with Grade-schoolers

Another step that will help move our children progressively toward praying on their own is "ping-pong prayers": we pray a prayer, our child prays a prayer, we pray a prayer, and so on. We should of course still discuss ahead of time the special things that we want to pray about or for. Our children can then cover those things in their prayers, and we can pray for other things we didn't discuss to give them examples of the kinds of things that they can pray about that are new to them. This is a great way to start introducing our children to the different things they can and should be praying about. (We'll cover teaching our children what to pray about in the next question.)

When our children are ready, the next step is to move them on to praying their entire prayers on their own. Depending on the child, we may want to make this change gradually. For example, we could alternate nights—one night ping-pong prayers and the next night saying their own prayers.

We should be careful at this point that, for the sake of a little extra time to ourselves in the evenings, we don't race off and leave our children praying on their own too soon. We need to stay with them for a while and listen to their prayers, continually encouraging them in the training process.

There are ways in which we can continue the training even after our children are praying on their own. Nights when it's late or when the kids are particularly tired, we can offer to say their prayers for them. This gives us the opportunity to lead them forward again by example. As our children get older, they'll begin to understand more and more how to talk to God about their feelings and intimate thoughts. They may feel hindered from praying this way when we're listening. We should respect their privacy and allow them to say their prayers, or part of their prayers, quietly to themselves while we sit and wait. We should also take the time to answer and/or discuss any questions that our children may have.

Praying with Preteens and Teenagers

When our children begin to want to pray entirely on their own, without us around at all, we should make sure that we're still available to them and that we help them structure their prayer time, perhaps scheduling that time to mesh with their bedtime. For example, if we want them in bed with the lights out at nine and they're currently spending twenty minutes reading their Bible and saying their prayers, they'll need to start the process by eight-forty.

It's especially important that we continue to talk to our older children about our own prayer life and the things that we're praying about. That openness will encourage them to talk to us about how things are going with *their* prayers. We need to look for every opportunity to continue the prayer training process so that it doesn't stagnate. With that goal in mind, we should continue to help our children identify and celebrate God's answers to their prayers.

All the way through this training process we should let our children know things that they can pray about for us and things that concern our family. This will help them know that their prayers are real, that their prayers make a difference, and that we value their prayers. We need to remember to thank our children for their prayers and tell them how things turned out when the answer comes.

The foundation of prayer is a relationship with God. Helping our children learn about and grow in prayer isn't like teaching them math or science—we're helping them get to know and learn to trust God. Relationships can't be forced; they need to grow and develop over time. If we relax and enjoy the process, so will our children.

What things should I be encouraging my children to pray about?

An easy way to explain to our kids what kinds of things they can and should talk to God about is to point out how they talk with us. We can divide conversation between us and them into two categories: casual conversation and practical conversation.

Casual conversation is talking about the weather and current events, about things that we're thinking or feeling. Casual conversation happens on the spur the moment and can be humorous, informational, or just plain as-it-happens chat.

Practical conversation has to do with things that *need* to be talked about—things that are essential and/or beneficial to running a household, working together as a family, and having a well-functioning parent-child relationship. These conversations cover things such as coordinating family schedules, checking to see if chores are done, finding out how school is going, reviewing report cards, planning a vacation, and talking about something that one of the kids needs.

This illustration is a great parallel to prayer and can be very helpful in explaining the contents of prayer to our children. Prayer is made up of both casual conversation and practical conversation with God—or casual prayer and practical prayer.

In *casual prayer* our children can talk to God about anything, anytime, anywhere. They can talk to him about how they feel, what they're thinking, what they're currently going through, what they're learning from the Bible, what their friends are up to, what their interests are. Every healthy relationship should have a casual-conversation element that's comfortable and growing; the same is true of prayer. We should encourage our children to spend some time talking to God about their thoughts and about what's going on in their lives, just as they do with us.

In *practical prayer* our children should talk to God about the things he wants people to talk to him about. Many topics for practical prayer are outlined by God in the Bible, just as parents generally choose the practical-conversation topics in a parent-child relationship. For example, the Bible says that we should pray for those who have authority over us—that is, our leaders:

> First, I want all of you to pray for everyone. Ask God to bless them. Give thanks for them. Pray for kings. Pray for all who are in authority. Pray that we will live peaceful and quiet lives. And pray that we will be godly and holy.
>
> (1 TIMOTHY 2:1–2)

For children, those in authority would include parents, teachers, church leaders, and political leaders. But praying for authority figures doesn't mean praying in vague generalities. Just as practical conversation in our home serves a specific purpose, so do practical prayers. In the verse above, we're told to pray for our leaders so that they may gain wisdom in making decisions that affect us, which is key to our living the life God wants us to live. Life, along with everything God created in and around it, works by prayer.

A good way to teach our children about practical prayers and help them understand some of the basics is to teach them the Lord's Prayer. When Jesus' disciples asked him to teach them how to pray, he responded by giving them the Lord's Prayer.

Although it's a great prayer to memorize and use in its original form, what Jesus was teaching his disciples went far beyond repeating the specific words. Jesus in effect taught us through this sample prayer how to pray, what our attitude should be in prayer, how we should approach God, and what we should talk to God about.

Here's a brief breakdown of some of the things that we can learn and teach our children from the Lord's Prayer (found in Matthew 6:9–13):

Our Father in heaven

- *The address:* Our children can go to God as their loving Father. They can also expand their opening by talking a little about God being their Father.
- *Example:* "Dear God, thank you for being my Father. Please help me have a good prayer time with you."

May your name be honored

- *Thank-you prayers:* We should help our children recognize, acknowledge, and thank God for his love and care. Affirming his goodness helps to strengthen their faith.
- *Example:* "Thank you for loving me and taking care of me. You're really great."

Your kingdom come

- *Church prayers:* We enter God's kingdom when we become his children. Jesus was showing us that we need to pray that more people will hear his story and become God's children. That involves praying for church leaders and workers and missionaries.
- *Example:* "Please help more and more people become your children. Let Uncle John know how much you love him. Give our church leaders wisdom so that they can help more people."

Your will be done on earth as it is in heaven

- *Prayers for leaders:* It is God's will that things on earth will work out according to his plan. So we pray for and about current events and world leaders as well as for our own leaders.
- *Example:* "Please give our politicians and all the voters wisdom about how to run our country."

Give us this day our daily bread

- *Special-to-me prayers:* This is where Jesus taught us to talk to God about our needs, our desires, and our concerns, about things that affect us and our lives personally. This is also where casual prayers come in.
- *Example:* "Thank you, God, for giving me a good school to go to. I'm really having a lot of fun. Help me make good friends. Also, could you help me do my best at math and understand it a little better?"

Forgive us our debts

- *Growing prayers:* The word *debts* here means the ways we've fallen short. Jesus was showing us that we need to talk to him about our personal growth, asking him to not only forgive us when we blow it but help us grow and learn to do things his way.

- *Example:* "I know that doing things your way is best. Help me learn more from my Bible and understand it better. I'm sorry for yelling at my brother today; please help me remember to talk gently and help us cooperate better."

As we forgive our debtors

- *Prayers for others:* Jesus taught us to pray for others—not just those who've hurt us or wronged us somehow, but those in our acquaintance who've fallen short (as we ourselves so often do).
- *Example:* "Could you help Ryan learn to cooperate with our teacher more? Also, please help Grandpa feel better. Thank you for answering my prayers for Cynthia; she's very nice to me now."

And do not lead us into temptation, but deliver us from the evil one

- *God's-way prayers:* Here Jesus was teaching us to talk to God about leading us, keeping us, and protecting us. We should pray for God's wisdom, guidance, and direction so that we can go his way and not the way of the evil one.
- *Example:* "God, could you please help me be wise and always make the right choices? I know that you love me and that you have good plans for me, so please keep me on your track."

For yours is the kingdom and the power and glory forever. Amen.

- *Closing:* When our children close, we should have them affirm that God has heard their prayers and will answer them according to his power and will.

- *Example:* "Thank you for hearing and answering my prayers. I know that you'll do what's best for me and for the people I pray for. Thank you! In Jesus name, Amen."

When our children are very young, their prayers can consist of an opening and a closing with thank-you prayers and special-to-me prayers sandwiched in between. As we take them further in the process, we can introduce more of the kinds of prayers represented in the Lord's Prayer. The most appropriate time to introduce a new type of prayer from the Lord's Prayer is when life gives us an opportunity to talk and pray about something in our children's lives that falls into one of the prayer categories. For example, if an election is going on and our children are asking about the process, this might be a good time to introduce prayers for leaders.

Here's an easy-to-memorize poem that will help young children learn and remember what the Lord's Prayer teaches us to pray:

THE THINGS I PRAY ABOUT

God and me	*[Address]*
and thank-yous many,	*[Thank-you prayers]*
I pray for the church	*[Church prayers]*
and leaders plenty;	*[Prayers for leaders]*
Things special to me	*[Special-to-me prayers]*
and help to grow,	*[Growing prayers]*
Then I pray for others	*[Prayers for others]*
and his way to go.	*[God's-way prayers]*
He hears my prayers	*[Closing]*
and answers them.	
And in Jesus' name	
I say Amen.	

This poem will be more helpful for some children than others. Some kids will benefit from it as merely a reminder of things to pray about, while others will want to use it as a template to guide them systematically through their prayers.

A final comment. For some children casual prayer may be the more difficult of the two types of conversation with God. For other children chatty conversation with God will come very easily. It all depends on their personality type. It's crucial that we not try to force our children into a certain prayer mold. Although it's important to have our children grow in both casual and practical prayer, it should be expected that some children will put a far greater emphasis on one than the other.

Are memorized prayers important, and are they effective?

Again, a good way to explain the answer to this question to your children is to draw a parallel with the conversations we have with each other. In everyday conversation we use many words, sentences, phrases, and even sets of sentences and phrases that we've memorized and simply repeat. For example, every time we see someone new in a day we exchange a fairly standard set of phrases: "Hello!" "Hi. How are you?" "I'm fine. And how are you?" "I'm well, thank you." And when someone says, "Thank you," our standard response is, "You're welcome." All these phrases are fine; indeed, it would be difficult to get by without them. But we can use them as a formula only, or we can say them from the heart and mean them. "How are you?" is sometimes a genuine question and sometimes nothing more than a routine phrase.

We also quote well-known lines and phrases that have come to mean a certain thing or are appropriate at certain points in a conversation; for example, "Don't shoot until you see the whites of their eyes" or "Three strikes and you're out." Sometimes these quotes are for the sake of humor; other times, since everyone understands their meaning and intent, they bring unity of understanding and help us get our point across. If we took those same phrases and threw them just anywhere in a conversation, in any context, they would neither make sense nor be appropriate. In fact, quoting memorized statements and phrases properly, appropriately, and in the right context takes as much thought as (or more thought than) just using our own words.

> If our entire time with God consisted of a long stream of memorized prayers and Bible verses or a single memorized prayer, our words would contain very little of ourselves. Using that sort of prayer, it would be difficult to talk about our thoughts and feelings with God and to develop an honest relationship.

Yet no matter how well-timed our quotes, if our entire conversation were a long string of memorized exchanges, humorous phrases, and famous quotes, people would begin to wonder if we ever had an original thought. An appropriate balance between our own words and "borrowed" words is necessary for true conversation—conversation that's sincere and that encourages relationship by revealing who we are and how we feel.

The same is true when we talk with God. We can have a certain way of opening our prayers and closing our prayers, or specific and repeated ways in which we pray about certain things. But if we stop thinking about what those standard elements mean and stop saying them sincerely, from the heart, they become meaningless.

We might also sometimes use memorized prayers that come from prayer books or from famous church leaders or from the Bible. If these are inserted in the right context and are used to express the true intent of our hearts and say what we truly want to say to or ask of God—then they add wonderfully to our prayer life. But if they're repeated as filler or as a set of magic words, they become flat and lifeless.

If our entire time with God consisted of a long stream of memorized prayers and Bible verses or a single memorized prayer, our words would contain very little of ourselves. Using that sort of prayer, it would be difficult to talk about our thoughts and feelings with God and to develop an honest relationship.

With our children this is especially true. As adults we can say a memorized prayer or quote a favorite Bible verse and do so with passion, perhaps remembering an experience or an emotion associated with the words. But children tend to concentrate on the memorized words and on getting them said. Younger children particularly have difficulty reflecting on memorized prayers while they're saying them.

But when used in context and in proper balance, memorized prayers can be a very helpful addition to a child's prayer life. When we introduce our children to a new prayer for memorization, we should first help them thoroughly understand what it means. We should also help them understand when to pray it: at those times when it expresses what they want to say to or ask of God.

Because practical prayers often have more structure than casual prayers, they lend themselves to being memorized and repeated. But even if our children use standard practical prayers, we can have them add fresh new thoughts and prayers about different people, items, and events. We can also encourage them to speak to God from the heart, without benefit of memorized prayers, when they're engaged in casual prayer with their Heavenly Father.

Younger children will often say the same prayers in the same way every night. There's no harm in this; it's quite natural.

We should, however, encourage them to think of one or two new prayers and new topics they can talk to God about each day. We should also encourage them to say their usual prayers slowly, reminding them that they're talking to a real person who's really listening.

How do I explain things to my children when their prayers aren't answered?

DAD, I'VE BEEN PRAYING FOR MONTHS ABOUT A CERTAIN TOY. ARE YOU SURE YOU DON'T HAVE AN OVERWHELMING DESIRE TO BUY ME SOMETHING EXPENSIVE?

DELUXE FULLY-OPERATIONAL CHILDREN'S JEEP

The best way to explain to our children how God answers or doesn't answer their prayers is to again draw a simple parallel between their asking us for things and their asking God for things.

There are basically three answers children can anticipate when asking parents for something: *yes*, which may come with some stipulation or adjustment to the original request; *no*, which is usually accompanied by one or more good reasons; and *maybe*, the category that most parental responses fall into.

- Our children make certain requests of us with the expectation of getting a *yes* answer—requests for things that they basically already know our will on. For instance, if we always let them have friends over on the weekend, let them watch a certain television show, allow them to have a snack at a certain time, or take them out for lunch after church, they'd anticipate a *yes* if they were to ask if things were going to be the same as usual. In the case of having friends over on the weekend, our kids might even tell their friends that they're sure it will be okay.
- Then there are requests that our kids fully expect to get a *no* answer to. For example, if it's an established family rule that we don't have friends over on school nights, or that no one turns the TV on until homework is done, or that a big bowl of ice cream after school isn't an acceptable snack, then if our kids asked us if we'd consider making an exception, they'd anticipate a *no*.
- Finally, there are a whole lot of requests that our children make of us that have *no predetermined* answer. Nothing in the past would help our kids anticipate with any certainty what our answer might be. They know that the answer could be either *yes* or *no*, depending on what kinds of things we consider in the decision-making process. For example, if a go-cart track had opened up a few miles from home and our children's friends had gone there and had a great time, our children might well ask us to take them there. If they knew that we often took the family out on special outings similar to this, they'd have reason to hope for a *yes*, although they couldn't be sure. After all, there might be factors that they're not aware of that would cause us to say *no* or *not yet*—factors such as the family budget, other plans for the weekend, or safety concerns. (We may, for example, have heard that a child was hurt riding these go-carts because the owners had cut some corners on safety.)

This parallel holds true when our children request things from God. There are many things outlined in the Bible that

God has already said he'll either give us or agree to. For example, God has told us again and again that he'll meet our basic needs—needs for food, clothing, shelter, and so on. And we know that he has instructed us, for our own good, to follow his principles—but he has also said that he'll help us learn to follow those principles. So if we ask God to help us always tell the truth, or be a better friend, or learn to say only kind things, or control our anger, we know that the answer is predetermined: it's *yes*. We'll call these prayers "*yes* prayers."

There are many *yes* prayers outlined in the Bible. As we've discussed, the Bible helps us know who God is, what he's like, and what he's willing to do. That's why getting to know and read our Bible is essential for developing a strong prayer life and a close relationship with God. As we get to know the Bible better, we'll know more about what we can ask God for and anticipate a *yes*.

But there are also requests to which we can anticipate receiving a definite *no* from God, as the Bible shows. We'll call these requests "*no* prayers." For example, the Bible says that God is love and that we're to forgive people who wrong us. Understanding that, we know that if we get really mad at someone and pray that God will punish him or her on our behalf, the answer will be *no*.

The majority of things that our children talk to God about fall into the same category as the majority of things they talk to us about: they're prayers that might get a *yes* answer or might get a *no* answer. We'll call them "*maybe* prayers." Occasionally the parallel breaks down here, unfortunately, because we're less than perfect as parents. Our children may ask us for something that's actually perfectly reasonable. Thinking just of them, we should give a *yes* answer, but the answer becomes *no* because to grant the request would greatly inconvenience us, or perhaps we're just too tired to do the work required of a *yes* response.

Whenever our children ask God for something reasonable and there's no reason that they shouldn't have it, the answer will be *yes*. But as in the go-cart example, there are many times that a *maybe* prayer receives a *no* answer or a *not yet* answer from God because he knows the bigger picture: he knows how the answer will affect us, he knows our life schedule, and he knows whether a *yes* answer to this request would take us in the wrong direction. He knows what's good for us and what isn't, and what's safe and what isn't. God hears and responds to every one of our *maybe* prayers, but we need to help our children realize that he answers according to his greater knowledge of who we are, where we are, and where we're going. But we can always be sure that his answer is in our best interest.

> God hears and responds to every one of our *maybe* prayers, but we need to help our children realize that he answers according to his greater knowledge of who we are, where we are, and where we're going. But we can always be sure that his answer is in our best interest.

At some point your children might wonder, If all of this is true, then why pray? Why not just let what's going to happen, happen? The parallel drawn earlier between your children asking you and them asking God will help you answer this question. Although your kids can trust you, if they never let you know what they wanted or expressed their interests and preferences, they'd end up missing out on a lot that you'd have been willing to give them if they'd talked to you about it.

Nothing gets by God. He knows what we need and desire, but because he gave us a will and wants a relationship with us in which we express our interests, preferences, and desires, he doesn't automatically do things in our life. The New Testament writer James sums it up by saying, "You don't have what you want, because you don't ask God" (James 4:2). When it comes to *yes* prayers and *maybe* prayers, God wants us to talk to him and ask him for things, and he wants to do the things that we'd like in our life. It's a partnership, a relationship.

That's the way God set it up, and that's the way he made it work. The more we talk to him and spend time getting to know him and letting him know what it is that we want and need, the more he does in our lives.

5

Angels and Heaven

∿∿∿∿∿∿∿∿∿∿∿∿∿∿∿∿∿∿∿∿∿∿∿∿

A. How can I answer my kids' questions about angels?

B. What can I tell my kids about heaven?

∿∿∿∿∿∿∿∿∿∿∿∿∿∿∿∿∿∿∿∿∿∿∿∿

How can I answer my kids' questions about angels?

Angels. Who doesn't get a warm and fuzzy feeling when talking about angels? And who doesn't get a million questions from the kids as soon as the topic comes up? It seems that we all, from youngest to oldest, have a tremendous curiosity about these spectacular beings and the place they inhabit in our imagination and dreams. No book on talking to your children about God would be complete without some mention of angels.

What Do Angels Look Like?

Angels have been depicted in many different ways over the centuries, from naked, chubby little children with small wings, to beautiful women with long flowing robes and large wings, to men dressed in white and glowing robes. Sometimes they've been depicted with halos, sometimes without; sometimes with harps, sometimes without; and sometimes even with Cupid's bow and arrows. There isn't much to learn about angels from these images, however—from artists' renderings, curio-store figurines, and characters in movies and television shows—except that the idea of angels inspires artists' imagination.

The book that contains stories, descriptions, and information about angels is the Bible, and that's where we should look when searching for answers to questions concerning these wonderful beings.

Every time angels appear in the Bible they appear as men. In some passages they're depicted as looking no different than ordinary men, but elsewhere they're described as majestic, awe-inspiring, and powerful in appearance. Although there's no biblical record of any angel appearing as a woman, gender isn't part of the essence of angels, as these words from Jesus reveal:

> At the resurrection people will neither marry nor be given in marriage; they will be like the angels in heaven.
>
> (MATTHEW 22:30, NIV)

Oddly enough, there is no mention anywhere in the Bible of angels having wings. Other fantastic creatures mentioned in the Bible, called *cherubim* and *seraphim*, are described as having wings, but these creatures are very different in appearance from the angels mentioned everywhere else in the Bible. They have more than one set of wings and also more than one face. Some people believe—and it's possible—that angels can take on more than one form and that they appear in the likeness of men only in order for us to be able to relate to them. Since the Bible isn't clear on this, it's probably better to assume that they look rather like us than to dress them up in fancy wings and such.

Nor is there any mention in the Bible of angels having halos. Halos were invented by artists as a way of depicting God's light or glory shining from angels and/or saints.

What Exactly Are Angels?

Many stories, especially those that have come to the big screen or television, have depicted angels as humans who've passed on from this world and are now back in a different form to assist us. Yet the Bible teaches that angels and humans are completely different, created differently and separately by God. Angels don't become humans and humans don't become angels. They're as different from each other as birds are from fish. Instead, angels are depicted in the Bible as powerful and majestic beings that live in God's presence and work in his service.

We need to be careful not to confuse how we treat truth and how we treat fiction with our children. Angels aren't in the same category as Tinkerbell and the tooth fairy, imaginary characters we can make up stories about to suit the moment. If we tell our kids that there's an angel behind every star, or that many angels can fit on the head of a pin, or that they themselves will become angels when they die, or that angels look like Cupid, or that Cupid is a real angel, our children will eventually question everything else we teach them about our faith.

> If we tell our kids that there's an angel behind every star, or that many angels can fit on the head of a pin, or that they themselves will become angels when they die, or that angels look like Cupid, or that Cupid is a real angel, our children will eventually question everything else we teach them about our faith.

When we're dealing with biblical information and truth—even about fantastic issues such as heaven and angels—it's important that we either give our children accurate answers or tell them that we don't know or aren't sure. And if we're not sure, we can look up with our children the various stories and verses in the Bible that mention angels and talk about the issue in that context. With our younger children, we can read all the stories in their Bible storybooks that mention angels.

What Do Angels Do? Do I Have an Angel?

The Bible tells us that God's angels do his bidding; they're sent by God to do things on behalf of us, his children. The Bible tells of angels bringing messages to God's children, protecting them, helping them escape impossible situations, bringing them food, strengthening them, and even fighting on their behalf. A verse in the New Testament book of Hebrews tells us to welcome strangers, adding, "By doing that, some people have welcomed angels without knowing it" (Hebrews 13:2).

The Bible doesn't clearly say whether or not each one of us has a guardian angel, or even if angels are constantly present. Angels *may* just show up as they're needed. On the other hand, since angels are beings in the spirit realm, where the dimensions of time and distance aren't a factor, the whole question might be moot. Regardless, our trust is to be in God, not in his angels. We can be confident that God's angels will act on our behalf when God has instructed them to do so. Angels don't act on their own initiative when it comes to their interactions with us; every example in the Bible depicts angels as strictly following God's instructions.

One verse in the Bible, a direct quote from Jesus, implies that children are looked after by angels, and that each child has a particular angel assigned to him or her. Jesus gave us so little information that it's impossible to nail down any exact details, but this verse of Scripture is the source of the concept of guardian angels (especially guardian angels for children):

See that you don't look down on one of these little ones. Here is what I tell you. Their angels in heaven can go at any time to see my father who is in heaven.

(MATTHEW 18:10)

When talking to our children about angels, our emphasis should be on God's care and love. Angels are awesome beings that deserve respect, and we'll be living alongside them eventually. But they're not greater than we are, and they shouldn't be worshiped or prayed to. Once, while having a vision, the Apostle John bowed down to worship an angel, but the angel told him not to, explaining that he and John were both servants of God.

Angels are not to be our children's invisible friends or guides. The only time people in the Bible talked to angels is when an angel showed up with a message from God—as, for example, when the angel Gabriel brought a message to Mary. These conversations always focused on God's will and message, never on the thoughts or opinions of the angel. It's *God* who is to be our children's ever-present friend and guide. He's the only one who can hear their prayers and help them always. Angels are only created beings like ourselves.

Talking about and teaching our children about angels can be interesting and faith-inspiring, but if we take our ideas and thoughts about angels beyond what the Bible says, we send the message to our kids that it's okay to speculate about spiritual things that aren't in the Bible. That can confuse our children as they get older and are exposed to a smorgasbord of spiritual ideas and theories that come from the human imagination without any basis in Scripture.

What can I tell my kids about heaven?

ARE GROUNDHOGS CALLED CLOUDHOGS WHEN THEY GET TO HEAVEN?

Children have a ton of questions about heaven. I guess the same is true for all of us—it's a fascinating topic. Throughout this book we've focused on getting to know God and following his principles as the key to a better life here on earth. And although this needs to be a focus for our children, we also need to let them know about the something better that's coming.

We live in a world that's broken, inhabited by people who are continuing to do things their way instead of following the guidebook for life. But ever since Adam and Eve moved out of the Garden of Eden, this world has been just a temporary home for humanity. The Bible tells us that this earth will be replaced with a new-and-improved, updated model when Jesus comes back at the end of this stage of world history.

Ever since the big move out of the Garden of Eden, we've all had a deep-seated desire for a perfect place to live, a perfect world—a desire for *home*. When we tell our children about how much God loves them and wants the best for them, the following question has to come up: "Why, then, are we living in this imperfect world polluted by hate, war, greed, and suffering?" We need to help our children understand that they'll live forever, and that their short stint here on earth is just the beginning of the awesome and wonderful plans God has for us. We may be stuck in an unfortunate stage of human history, but it's just for a short time when seen in the perspective of God's eternal plans for us.

Yes, God wants to give our children the best possible life here on earth. But we should help them look forward to the rest of their life, in eternity, where things will be incredible, where there will be no sadness, crying, war, death, or suffering, but only good and awesome experiences and opportunities. The hope for a better place and an eternity with God can give our children the extra encouragement they need to keep on doing things God's way, even when the going gets tough.

When we consider eternity with God and his plans for us as his children, the sixty or eighty or a hundred years spent here on earth hardly seem to deserve the attention we give them. But the years here are important—not because they're all there is, but because they're a preparation for and the beginning of an eternally growing relationship with God.

What Will Heaven Be Like?

The Bible tells us very little about what heaven will be like, but what it does tell us is exciting enough. Jesus spoke about the "kingdom of heaven." We enter that kingdom when we become God's children. We're then under his authority and care forever. As we trust and follow him, we can experience his love right here and now; and the Bible teaches us that when we, as God's children, die, we'll go to be with the Father.

That place isn't really described in the Bible, but we know that we'll enter into the spiritual realm, where God is.

Jesus told us that he was going to prepare a special place for us, an awesome place where we can be with him:

> There are many rooms in my Father's house. If this were not true, I would have told you. I am going there to prepare a place for you. If I go and do that, I will come back. And I will take you to be with me. Then you will also be where I am.
>
> (JOHN 14:2–3)

That place Jesus is preparing is the place where we'll go with him after he returns to earth.

Other passages in the Bible teach that after the second coming of Jesus, God is going to remodel, and we'll receive an all-new heaven and earth. The book of Revelation talks about the phenomenal place this will be:

> I heard a loud voice from the throne. It said, "Now God makes his home with human beings. He will live with them. They will be his people. And God himself will be with them and be their God. He will wipe away every tear from their eyes. There will be no more death or sadness. There will be no more crying or pain. Things are no longer the way they used to be.
>
> (REVELATION 21:3–4)

Whether we're talking about the kingdom of heaven to which we belong now, or the place we'll go to when we die, or the realm we'll live in at the end of this age, the common elements are God's care and presence and our relationship with him. The scenery may change as we go from life to death and from one age to the next, but the ultimate privilege and joy of knowing God and experiencing his love will only get better and better as we draw closer to him. And we can trust that whatever God has in store for us will always be beyond our expectations.

The key features of heaven, then, are our relationship with God and our receiving his love, care, blessings, and goodness—features that start not after death but when we become God's children and begin the process of getting to know him daily.

When we talk to our children about heaven, we can tell them what a great place it will be, but the emphasis should always be on *why* it will be so phenomenal: heaven will be great because we'll be even more directly in God's presence and in his care. With that emphasis we can help our kids understand that they're citizens of heaven *now*. In the following verse, which is often quoted as talking about heaven, the Apostle Paul is talking about much more than the hereafter; he's talking about *everything* involved in being a Christian, from becoming God's child to the far reaches of eternity:

> It is written, "No eye has seen, no ear has heard, no mind has known what God has prepared for those who love him."
>
> (1 CORINTHIANS 2:9)

Who Gets to Go to Heaven?

This is actually a far easier question to answer for your children than you might think at first. Jesus died in our place. He took the penalty for our sins. And his death opened the way for all people—each and every human being everywhere—to be able to make the choice again as to whether they'll trust God as their Father and receive his love, care, teaching, guidance, and direction for their lives. When we believe and decide to trust God, we become God's children and citizens of the kingdom of heaven forever:

> When you sin, the pay you get is death. But God gives you the gift of eternal life because of what Christ Jesus our Lord has done.
>
> (ROMANS 6:23)

What is love? It is not that we loved God. It is that he loved
us and sent his Son to give his life to pay for our sins.

(1 JOHN 4:10)

God loved the world so much that he gave his one and only
Son. Anyone who believes in him will not die but will have
eternal life.

(JOHN 3:16)

God is merciful, and it's his desire that every one of us will
end up spending eternity with him:

God did not send his Son into the world to judge the world.
He sent his Son to save the world through him.

(JOHN 3:17)

The Lord is not slow to keep his promise. He is not slow the
way some people understand it. He is patient with you. He
doesn't want anyone to be destroyed. Instead, he wants all
people to turn away from their sins.

(2 PETER 3:9)

Although the price has been paid, each person still has an
individual will and needs to make a choice. From the beginning God has honored the right he gave us to make a choice.
Those who choose to trust God as their Father and accept
what Jesus did for them will definitely enter the kingdom of
heaven:

Say with your mouth, "Jesus is Lord." Believe in your heart
that God raised him from the dead. Then you will be saved.

(ROMANS 10:9)

If our kids did something wrong and knew that we weren't
too pleased with them, what would they need to do? To make
things right, they'd need to come to us and say they were
sorry. When our children come to the place where they know

that they believe in God and in what Jesus did, they simply need to go to God (just as they'd come to us). In prayer they can ask God to forgive them because Jesus died in their place, and they can ask him to start being their Father.

> Sometimes we think that Jesus wanted only those people to be Christians who look like us, act like us, think like us, and so on. But Jesus didn't add all that stuff to the requirement; *we* did. Jesus took becoming God's child down to one simple thing: accepting God's free gift of forgiveness delivered via the death of his Son.

Our children can become Christians—in other words, make things right with their Father—in many unique ways, just as our own children would go about making things right with us each in his or her own way. If you were to ask a roomful of Christians how they came to God, you'd get a wide range of responses. Some people would be able to say exactly when they first believed and decided; others would say that the commitment grew over a period of time. Our children may make their decision during a service at church, during private prayer, in family devotions, at a youth gathering, or on a walk; they may react with overwhelming emotion or respond with matter-of-fact conviction. While the variables are many, the key is universal: they will believe and decide and begin a relationship with their Father. It's as simple as that.

The question often comes up in today's world, "Isn't it a little exclusive and perhaps narrow-minded to say that only those who believe in God through Jesus are accepted?" We need to help our children understand that Christianity isn't exclusive; on the contrary, it's incredibly *in*clusive.

Jesus said that he was the only way to the Father: "I am the way and the truth and the life. No one comes to the Father except through me" (John 14:6). If we believe that Jesus spoke the truth and that the Bible is God's book, we can't contradict his words and say that there are many ways to God. But we should look at Jesus' motivation for saying what he said. Sometimes we think that Jesus wanted only those people to be Christians who look like us, act like us, think like us, and so on. In fact, when we think of what a Christian should be, we sometimes get such a detailed image that we know what even the *haircut* should look like! But Jesus didn't add all that stuff to the requirement; *we* did. Jesus took becoming God's child down to one simple thing: accepting God's free gift of forgiveness delivered via the death of his Son.

Jesus not only made it simple and inclusive, he made it possible. No one can become a child of God through individual merit, intelligence, or goodness, because no one is good enough or smart enough! We can come to God only through his grace and forgiveness—and those things come through Jesus' death. Jesus wasn't narrowing the gates of heaven; he was swinging them wide open. *No one* could make it in before he paid the price, but now *anyone*, anywhere, no matter what, can get in.

Jesus not only made it simple and possible, he made it clear. Parents who love their children spend whatever time is needed to teach and train them, letting them know how life works best and how to get through it. If we were to advise our children, "Hey, just do whatever you want and hope it turns out," we wouldn't be very good parents. Because God is a good parent who loves us, he made the road to himself as clear and straightforward as possible. He doesn't just say, "Hey, wing it, and you might find me."

Before Jesus lived on this earth, every religious form was exclusive, demanding exact conformity right down to race and culture. The route to enlightenment was complicated and uncertain. Then Jesus came and announced an inclusive, possible, simple, clear, and absolutely certain way to become God's child so that anyone and everyone could understand the message and come to receive God's love and life.

No matter who people are, or where they are in the world, or what culture or religion they were brought up in, if they recognize that they need God's help and that they can't please him on their own, God will meet them. Jesus paid the price so that *all* people could come in to the kingdom.

When we teach our children that Jesus is the only way, we need to be careful that they don't take that to mean that everyone in the world needs to look and act a certain way in order to please God. But we also need to let them know that the essence of the Christian message is simple: Jesus is the wide-open door to heaven through which *anyone* can enter and through which everyone must enter.

> **Helping our children understand the inclusiveness of the gospel should help them become more accepting of other cultures and people.**

Helping our children understand the inclusiveness of the gospel should help them become more accepting of other cultures and people. *Anyone* and *everyone* can come! We should be careful to explain, too, that God wants us to respect other people's right to believe and live the way they want to, as God himself does. We should always treat others, no matter what they believe or how they live, with love and respect, and we shouldn't think that we're better than they are. We're God's children because Jesus died for us, not because we're intelligent or good or because we figured out how to get right with God. We merely heard, believed, and decided.

And finally, we should help our children understand that although God wants us to tell others about his love, he hasn't given us the right to judge others or to decide who's going to heaven; that's God's job. And it's a good thing it *is* his job—he's a merciful judge.

Conclusion

Can we be sure our prayers and efforts will help?

We started this book talking about our comfort level in discussing our spiritual life and our religion. Since then we've covered a lot of territory and made many suggestions about how to help our children grow spiritually, develop a wonderful relationship with God, and receive his love.

At this point we may wonder whether or not we can do all that's required—and whether or not it will be effective. None of us is perfect as a parent, and most of us already have a lot on our parenting plates (not to mention all of our other plates).

But there's hope! The key to spiritual parenting is also the key to taking the stress out of spiritual parenting. God loves our children more than we can possibly imagine, and he wants them to develop a relationship with him and receive his love. He wants them to be the best possible people they can be, and he wants to see them have the best possible life and eternity that they can have. He really *is* their Father, their parent, and he will be—forever. He's given us the honor and privilege of being able to bring his children into this world and help in teaching and training them, but it's *his* life and training program; he invented it, and he's the one who really knows our kids and knows what's in store for them for the rest of eternity.

Human beings are the most intricate, complicated, and phenomenal creatures of all. Scientists, doctors, theologians, philosophers, and psychologists have invested lifetimes trying to understand the wonders of the human body, mind, and spirit. They've discovered volumes upon volumes of fascinating data and insights, but all would agree that we haven't even scratched the surface. The idea that God would turn these awesome creatures over to something called parents—people who don't have a clue!—is daunting, but it's absurd and unthinkable that God would do so without the intention of working with these parents, training them, and actually helping them get the job done.

Therefore, we can relax in the process and trust that God is on the job. Parenting won't happen automatically, however; God won't just do it for us. It's part of God's program and of his original design to partner with parents in the parenting process. He's given us a privilege and a responsibility—and we again have a will, a choice, that God will honor. So when we as parents turn to God and decide to bring our kids up in relationship with him and in partnership with him, and we ask him for help and wisdom, he's motivated, ready, willing, and able to work with us and help us get the job done.

When we bring our children up in a way that's in harmony with everything God created—according to the manufacturer's instructions, as it were, and with his toll-free help-line constantly open—we have the greatest possibility for success. Yes, our children's wills are involved, but God wired our children for a relationship with him, and he's given us the best way to raise our children—in harmony with his principles and in partnership with him. If we raise our children his way and with his help, then we'll get the best results.

Another very important, helpful, and encouraging thing to remember is that God is always with our children. When we trust him to help in the parenting process, he not only works with us and helps us; he works directly with our children as well, working in their hearts and minds and circumstances, teaching them, giving them help, wisdom, and guidance continually.

The key to spiritual parenting, then, in a nutshell, is to relax and learn to trust God to help give us the words, wisdom, and ideas as we need them, and to work in the minds, hearts, and lives of our children. We must pray for our children and our parenting skills daily. And when the going gets tough, we need to keep on praying and keep on trusting. After all, we're working with the manufacturer; he knows what he's doing.

Our children's spiritual life and relationship with God is a journey, and so is the spiritual parenting process. It's a step-by-step, day-by-day process for us in parenting and for our children in growing and learning. We'll make mistakes, and our kids will blow it; it's inevitable. So we need to relax, ask God for wisdom and help, and slowly work our way through and past the difficulties. God doesn't expect us to be perfect; he just wants, for our sakes, to make sure we keep moving toward perfection. And when we trust God to partner with us, he complements us perfectly and compensates for our short-comings. He knows that we can't do it perfectly on our own—but then he didn't intend for us to do it without him!

You can reach Rick Osborne at:

Lightwave Publishing
Box 160
Maple Ridge, BC
Canada V2X 7G1

Or on the Internet at:
http://www.lightwavepublishing.com